CO-AYL-352

Christopher J. Alexander, PhD
Editor

Working with Gay Men and Lesbians in Private Psychotherapy Practice

Working with Gay Men and Lesbians in Private Psychotherapy Practice has been co-published as *Journal of Gay & Lesbian Social Services*, Volume 8, Number 4 1998.

Pre-publication
REVIEWS,
COMMENTARIES,
EVALUATIONS . . .

"**T**his collection is rich with information that will prove especially invaluable to therapists planning to or recently having begun to work with lesbian and gay clients in private practice. Yet, it contains thoughtful information for experienced clinicians in this area, notably for helpful insight into working with people of color and the practical aspects of managing a private practice."

Michael Shernoff, MSW
Private Practice, NYC
Adjunct Faculty, Hunter College
Graduate School of Social Work

Working with Gay Men and Lesbians in Private Psychotherapy Practice

Working with Gay Men and Lesbians in Private Psychotherapy Practice has been co-published as *Journal of Gay & Lesbian Social Services*, Volume 8, Number 4 1998.

Working with Gay Men and Lesbians in Private Psychotherapy Practice

Christopher J. Alexander, PhD
Editor

Working with Gay Men and Lesbians in Private Psychotherapy Practice, edited by Christopher J. Alexander, was co-published by The Haworth Press, Inc., under the same title, as a special issue of *Journal of Gay & Lesbian Social Services*, Volume 8, Number 4 1998, James J. Kelly, Editor.

Harrington Park Press
An Imprint of
The Haworth Press, Inc.
New York • London

1-56023-125-4

Published by

Harrington Park Press, 10 Alice Street, Binghamton, NY 13904-1580 USA

Harrington Park Press is an imprint of The Haworth Press, Inc., 10 Alice Street, Binghamton, NY 13904-1580 USA.

Working with Gay Men and Lesbians in Private Psychotherapy Practice has been co-published as *Journal of Gay & Lesbian Social Services* ™, Volume 8, Number 4 1998.

Cover design by Jennifer M. Gaska

Library of Congress Cataloging-in-Publication Data

Working with gay men and lesbians in private psychotherapy practice / Christopher J. Alexander, editor.
     p. cm.
     "Co-published as Journal of gay & lesbian social services, volume 8, number 4, 1998."
     Includes bibliographical references and index.
     ISBN 0-7890-0693-6 (alk. paper) ISBN 1-56023-125-4 (pbk.: alk. paper)
     1. Gays–Mental health services. 2. Gays–Mental health. 3. Psychotherapist and patient. I. Alexander, Christopher J. II. Journal of gay & lesbian social services, v. 8, no. 4.

RC451.4.G39W67 1998
616.89′14′068–dc21
                                            98-48951
                                             CIP

INDEXING & ABSTRACTING

Contributions to this publication are selectively indexed or abstracted in print, electronic, online, or CD-ROM version(s) of the reference tools and information services listed below. This list is current as of the copyright date of this publication. See the end of this section for additional notes.

- *AIDS Newsletter c/o CAB International/CAB ACCESS*
- *Cambridge Scientific Abstracts*
- *caredata CD: the social and community care database*
- *CNPIEC Reference Guide: Chinese National Directory of Foreign Periodicals*
- *Contemporary Women's Issues*
- *Criminal Justice Abstracts*
- *Digest of Neurology and Psychiatry*
- *ERIC Clearinghouse on Urban Education (ERIC/CUE)*
- *Family Studies Database (online and CD/ROM)*
- *HOMODOK/"Relevant" Bibliographic Database*
- *IBZ International Bibliography of Periodical Literature*
- *Index to Periodical Articles Related to Law*
- *INTERNET ACCESS (& additional networks) Bulletin Board for Libraries ("BUBL"), coverage of information resources on INTERNET, JANET, and other networks.*
- *Mental Health Abstracts (online through DIALOG)*
- *Referativnyi Zhurnal (Abstracts Journal of the All-Russian Institute of Scientific and Technical Information)*
- *Social Work Abstracts*
- *Sociological Abstracts (SA)*
- *Studies on Women Abstracts*
- *Violence and Abuse Abstracts: A Review of Current Literature on Interpersonal Violence (VAA)*

(continued)

Special Bibliographic Notes related to special journal issues
(separates) and indexing/abstracting

- indexing/abstracting services in this list will also cover material in any "separate" that is co-published simultaneously with Haworth's special thematic journal issue or DocuSerial. Indexing/abstracting usually covers material at the article/chapter level.

- monographic co-editions are intended for either non-subscribers or libraries which intend to purchase a second copy for their circulating collections.

- monographic co-editions are reported to all jobbers/wholesalers/approval plans. The source journal is listed as the "series" to assist the prevention of duplicate purchasing in the same manner utilized for books-in-series.

- to facilitate user/access services all indexing/abstracting services are encouraged to utilize the co-indexing entry note indicated at the bottom of the first page of each article/chapter/contribution.

- this is intended to assist a library user of any reference tool (whether print, electronic, online, or CD-ROM) to locate the monographic version if the library has purchased this version but not a subscription to the source journal.

- individual articles/chapters in any Haworth publication are also available through the Haworth Document Delivery Service (HDDS).

CONTENTS

ABOUT THE EDITOR

Christopher J. Alexander, PhD, is a licensed clinical psychologist. He maintains private psychotherapy practices in Santa Fe, and Las Cruces, New Mexico. He is author of *Growth and Intimacy for Gay Men: A Workbook* and editor of *Gay and Lesbian Mental Health: A Sourcebook for Practitioners*, both published by The Haworth Press, Inc. Dr. Alexander is on the editorial board of the *Journal of Homosexuality* and Contributing Editor to the *Journal of Gay & Lesbian Social Services* (both Haworth Press journals).

Feedback regarding this book, as well as general questions on gay male mental health, may be directed to Dr. Alexander at 620-B West San Francisco Street, Santa Fe, NM 87501.

Foreword

Though it seems like only yesterday, it has been fifteen years since I opened my private practice with the intent of serving the mental health needs of the lesbian, gay, bisexual, and transgendered communities. A sampling of cases from my first six months in practice included several gay men attempting to overcome the psychological damage resulting from failed attempts at "reparative" therapy, a lesbian couple with two young children attempting to deal with issues of combined families, an African-American man who had been previously (and inappropriately) diagnosed as borderline because of his feelings of exclusion and anger at both the gay and African-American communities, and a number of lesbians and gay men ranging in age from adolescence to their sixties who were struggling with issues of coming out. These cases presented issues with which I had varying degrees of experience and familiarity. I felt even less grounded with the male-to-female transsexual requesting a psychological evaluation in prepara-

---

Douglas C. Haldeman, PhD, is a Counseling Psychologist in private practice in Seattle, Washington. He is Clinical Professor of Psychology at the University of Washington and Clinical Instructor in the Counselor Preparation program at Seattle University. Dr. Haldeman is the author of numerous journal articles and book chapters on psychotherapy with lesbians, gay men, and bisexuals, and has written and lectured extensively on the implications of sexual orientation conversion therapies. He is co-author of the American Psychological Association's policy on "Appropriate Therapeutic Responses to Sexual Orientation," and is past chair of APA's Committee on Lesbian, Gay and Bisexual Concerns, and Past President of APA's Society for the Psychological Study of Lesbian, Gay and Bisexual Issues. He and his partner of twenty years reside in Seattle, and are breeders of many champion Samoyeds.

Address correspondence to: Douglas C. Haldeman, 2910 East Madison, Suite 302, Seattle, WA 98112.

[Haworth co-indexing entry note]: "Foreword." Haldeman, Douglas C. Co-published simultaneously in *Journal of Gay & Lesbian Social Services* (The Haworth Press, Inc.) Vol. 8, No. 4, 1998, pp. xvii-xxii; and: *Working with Gay Men and Lesbians in Private Psychotherapy Practice* (ed: Christopher J. Alexander) The Haworth Press, Inc., 1998, pp. xiii-xviii. Single or multiple copies of this article are available for a fee from The Haworth Document Delivery Service [1-800-342-9678, 9:00 a.m. - 5:00 p.m. (EST). E-mail address: getinfo@haworthpressinc.com].

xii   Working with Gay Men and Lesbians in Private Psychotherapy Practice

tion for gender reassignment surgery, or with the bisexual man whose initial task with me was to discover whether or not I believed that bisexuality actually existed, or if I felt, as previous therapists had, that he was simply a gay man clutching the last vestiges of his denial.

I came to private practice with life experience as a gay man, but also having done a pre-doctoral internship at an l/g/b/t community mental health agency, and a dissertation (much to the consternation of some of my committee members) on the social and psychological effects of sexual dysfunction in gay men. Nevertheless, in 1983, the current fountain of relevant information for practitioners working with l/g/b/t individuals was but a trickle. With some client populations, and with some issues, I felt myself to be on less than terra firma with regard to scope of practice issues. Nevertheless, I remember wondering, "If I do not see this individual, who will?," fully aware that many presenting for therapy at that time were attempting to undo the damage done by previous treatments.

There was one core certainty in 1983, however, which remains unchanged today: that same-gender sexual orientation in and of itself does not constitute a form of mental illness, nor a predisposition to social or psychological maladaption, nor a diminishment in role competence as a spouse, parent, worker, friend, or family member. The scientific database supporting the decision of the major mental health organizations to remove homosexuality from its previously inappropriate inclusion in the taxonomy of mental illnesses has only grown in the past twenty-five years. There are still, of course, fringe coalitions of professionals, supported by the political far right and Christian fundamentalists, who would attempt to persuade society that same-gender sexual orientation is an illness which is freely chosen from life's behavioral menu. Nevertheless, from the standpoint of organized mental health, the issue has long been settled.

So if we do not treat same-gender sexual orientation as an illness, how do we respond therapeutically? The first evidence of bias in psychotherapy with lesbians and gay men came in a 1991 report by the American Psychological Association's Committee on Lesbian and Gay Concerns. This report revealed a wide range of therapeutic practice with lesbian and gay psychotherapy clients, and suggested a number of themes reflective of both inappropriate and exemplary practice.

As a clinical instructor responsible for educating graduate students and interns on issues pertinent to assessment and intervention with l/g/b clients, I have found this document to be an invaluable resource. Moreover, it serves as the foundation upon which the APA's Society for the Psychological Study of Lesbian, Gay and Bisexual Issues (Division 44) and the Committee on Lesbian, Gay and Bisexual Concerns are developing guidelines for assessment, training, and psychotherapy with l/g/b clients. This important work will provide much-needed content with respect to the question of what constitutes competent clinical practice with these populations, and will serve l/g/b and non-l/g/b practitioners alike, as well as those who train them. We are, after all, more likely than our heterosexual counterparts to seek the services of a psychotherapist. We inhabit urban areas, many of which are blessed with a plethora of "out" practitioners, and rural areas in which there may be no l/g/b practitioners, or even individuals with any training in this area at all. It is therefore incumbent upon all clinicians to have at least some passing familiarity with our issues.

Editor Christopher Alexander, in his paper "Treatment Planning for Gay and Lesbian Clients," outlines a practical guide for the planning and treatment of l/g/b clients. In addition to those issues common to the process of treatment planning with non-gay clients, Alexander points out the questions unique to treatment planning with lesbians and gay men: Does the therapist disclose her/his own sexual orientation? How does the therapist assess the client's concerns about the process of therapy in general, and/or the therapist's view of and expertise in sexual orientation issues? How does the therapist address the degree to which internalized stigma about sexual orientation may impact the client's ability to set, or work toward, goals of a personal or professional nature? Alexander also addresses the special complexities introduced into psychotherapy by managed care. Confidentiality issues are especially relevant here, as are the variability in managed care companies ensuring of l/g/b-sensitive practitioners' inclusion on their panels.

There are numerous issues relevant for practitioners working with l/g/b clients which are not covered by practice guidelines. Many of these issues are embedded in theoretical concerns, or in the social phenomenology of the therapy process and its uniquenesses with l/g/b clients of all ethnic identities and family configurations, and the special features of l/g/b communities. As such, there may be few definitive answers; nonetheless, it is important that we be aware of the questions involved, their complexities, and the fact that as our field changes, so do the questions.

One needs only to read Joel Frost's comprehensive review and recommendations for "Staying Current with Gay and Lesbian Research and Practice Knowledge" to get a sense of the tremendous growth in our field. Frost addresses developments in theoretical understanding of sexual orientation, and provides a wealth of literature for resource information. The review includes references on a variety of other content areas, including HIV/AIDS, internalized shame and homophobia, lesbian/gay couples, and aging. Further, Frost offers the practitioner specific professional and community-based resources.

Early work in our field was affected by some of the same research biases that permeate mainstream psychological study: that what is relevant to the lives of affluent white gay men is not necessarily applicable to lesbians, bisexual men and bisexual women, and all ethnic minority l/g/b individuals. One important objective of l/g/b-affirmative psychology has been to disseminate accurate information about sexual orientation, and the normative life experiences of l/g/b individuals, to society at large. But if we are to do this, we must first understand each other, and the multiple identities inherent in all l/g/b communities.

To this end, this collection includes an important and thoughtful reflection by Richard Rodriguez on "Clinical and Practical Considerations in Private Practice with Lesbians and Gay Men of Color." Rodriguez raises a number of important considerations in a heretofore understudied area. The interface of clinical issues in psychotherapy, such as coming out, multiple identity and gender role, and issues particular to culture and ethnicity, such as language, cultural implications of multiple identity and identity development, spirituality, gender roles, and the multiplicity of sources of oppression, must be carefully considered by the therapist seeking to work competently and ethically with l/g/b clients of color. To the untrained or insensitive non-minority practitioner, normative responses to any of these issues may be incorrectly perceived as evidence of personality pathology. Practitioners, particularly those working without direct connection to academic settings, need to appreciate and understand these concerns, along with the context of class and racism in which ethnic minority clients' therapeutic issues are invariably embedded.

Rodriguez also raises the question of boundary issues as they apply to therapeutic relationships with l/g/b clients. He points out, as do Jim Fickey and Gary Grimm in their article, "Boundary Issues in Gay and Lesbian Psychotherapy Relationships," that the possible multiple roles for therapist and client (community worker/activist, relation in social circles, etc.) may pose special challenges for the therapuetic relationship. Fickey and Grimm offer a comprehensive discussion of the complexities involved with the therapist's decision as to whether or not to come out, as well as other issues which may be relevant in the transference and countertransference of the therapuetic relationship. Further, issues of dual relationship, both during and after therapy, are of particular concern for therapists in small towns and big cities alike (since the l/g/b communities in the latter so often seem like the former).

Boundary issues are among those addressed in Pamm Hanson and Pamela Weeks' discussion of therapeutic and practical considerations for lesbian therapists and their clients. These authors offer a thorough discussion of issues relative to the structure of therapeutic practice, raising a number of concerns both theoretical and practical. Given the "close" feeling of l/g/b communities, even in large cities, the authors take up questions related to chance public encounters between therapist and client; political and personal activities and connections of both parties which may bring them together outside the therapy office; and theoretical issues of power, economics and boundaries.

Last, but certainly not least, we face the reality that most of us apprehended only after training: that private practice is a business. As most of us in this field are not natural-born or self-identified entrepreneurs, Christopher Alexander's article, "The Business of Private Practice: Marketing Strategies for Gay and Lesbian Therapists," will offer not only the permission and encouragement to "think like a businessperson," but will offer a strategic plan for establishing, marketing, and developing a private practice in l/g/b psychology. This plan includes a number of specific suggestions on getting started (and keeping going), and is applicable to practitioners in any number of demographic and geographic settings.

While elucidating many of the questions that we are only beginning to address, the present work serves as testament to the tremendous breadth and depth that the practice of gay-affirmative psychotherapy has achieved in the past twenty-five years. Rich in thought-provoking questions and challenges, and full of specific suggestions for the practitioner who works with l/g/b clients, this special volume will be useful for the practitioner and those wishing to become better informed about the implications of competent practice with these populations. The variety of issues discussed here truly signals our readiness as a practice and science for increased visibility as a profession. For the private practitioner working with l/g/b clients, the opportunities for contribution will be limitless.

Douglas C. Haldeman, PhD
Past President
Society for the Psychological Study of Lesbian,
Gay, and Bisexual Issues

Introduction

Christopher J. Alexander

In 1989 I was doing my pre-doctoral internship at a family service agency in Northern California. Like many agencies that rely upon the assistance of interns, this facility offered affordable mental health care to residents of the community. In exchange for the individual and group supervision I received, I had the responsibility of maintaining a caseload of five to nine clients. Since I was the only trainee interested in working with children, most of my clients were young boys and girls, brought to therapy by their parents to help them cope with divorce, trauma, and other significant life changes.

One day, my supervisor approached me regarding a case. A man had phoned asking if we work with gay couples. My supervisor assured him that we do, and she gave the case to me. The decision to give me the case was based solely on the fact I am gay. Though I had worked extensively with gay men in my role as a social worker at the San Francisco AIDS Foundation, this was a new challenge. For the first time in my training and career, I was being relied upon to help a couple of twelve years work through the myriad of communication and trust issues of their relationship.

Naturally, I felt excited and challenged by this opportunity. Never before had I done intensive, on-going work with any couples, let alone two gay men. The work I did with them made me aware that issues

Christopher J. Alexander, PhD, is a licensed clinical psychologist in Santa Fe, NM. He is author of *Growth and Intimacy for Gay Men: A Workbook* and editor of *Gay and Lesbian Mental Health: A Sourcebook for Practitioners*. He can be reached at 620-B W. San Francisco Street, Santa Fe, NM 87501.

[Haworth co-indexing entry note]: "Introduction." Alexander, Christopher J. Co-published simultaneously in *Journal of Gay & Lesbian Social Services* (The Haworth Press, Inc.) Vol. 8, No. 4, 1998, pp. 1-3; and: *Working with Gay Men and Lesbians in Private Psychotherapy Practice* (ed: Christopher J. Alexander) The Haworth Press, Inc., 1998, pp. 1-3. Single or multiple copies of this article are available for a fee from The Haworth Document Delivery Service [1-800-342-9678, 9:00 a.m. - 5:00 p.m. (EST). E-mail address: getinfo@haworthpressinc.com].

couples face are often the same, regardless of the sexual orientation of the two people. Simultaneously, I also came to understand that being a sexual minority does exert unique influences on a relationship. Sorting these two factors out was an incredible challenge, and naturally I turned to my supervisor for guidance on how to best work with these two men.

To her credit, my supervisor told me that she didn't know much about gay men or gay couples. Later, when I transferred these two men to my caseload at my next internship, my new supervisor said the same thing. In short, I was confronted with having to apply traditional systems theory and approach to my work with this couple, while deciding how best to make sense out of the sexual orientation concerns influencing their relationship.

I don't fault either supervisor for not knowing how to coach me in my work with this couple. I appreciate their honesty in telling me of their limited experience in working with gay men, and I am grateful to both for permitting me to work with these men in light of the circumstances. But much of what I have addressed thus far raises a very crucial issue for those of us who choose to work with gay men or lesbians in private practice. Specifically, each of us must account for what training and specialized knowledge we have that makes us an appropriate choice for the gay and lesbian mental health services consumer.

PRIVATE PRACTICE AS A UNIQUE ROLE

When states grant us a license to practice psychology, counseling or social work, they in essence are saying that we are competent, by education and experience, to work independently. Aside from the requirement many states have that licensed mental health professionals receive continuing education, most clinicians are able to see and work with whomever they desire. Inherent in this is an honor system that trusts us to only provide services for which we're thoroughly trained.

As Joel Frost discusses in this volume, there are no clear guidelines that specify who is and is not qualified to work with sexual minorities. Often, gays and lesbians assume any licensed mental health professional is able to provide them with adequate services. Many gay and lesbian health care professionals, however, cringe at this notion. But are clinicians who identify as gay or lesbian better qualified, on the basis of life experience, to work with sexual minorities?

Because of the education and training I have received, I feel I am an ethical and competent private practitioner. In my practice, I provide a variety of services, and I work with a diverse group of people. Yet, if you were to examine my professional training, you would see that most of my supervised experience is in the field of child psychology. So what makes me qualified to work with the gay men and lesbians I see in my private practice?

These are not easy questions for us to answer. Private practitioners, regardless of who we work with or how we provide treatment, are in a unique role. Unlike many jobs which require specialized experience and familiarity with the duties to be performed, the assumption is that those of us who work privately know what we are doing and how best to work with the clients on our caseload.

This collection of articles attempts to tackle some of the particular challenges gay and lesbian private practitioners confront. Though there are books and articles which cover specific issues gays and lesbians must sometimes deal with (relationships, dating, coming out, AIDS, etc.), very few of these speak to the concerns of the gay or lesbian mental health professional who has a private practice. This collection, therefore, is an attempt to fill this void by offering readers practical and useful strategies they can build into their work with gay and lesbian clients.

The men and women who have contributed to this volume are all licensed mental health professionals, each of whom currently maintains a full or part time private practice. Further, each contributor specializes in the treatment of gay men or lesbians, in addition to other professional commitments.

Staying Current
with Gay and Lesbian Research
and Practice Knowledge

Joel C. Frost

SUMMARY. The field of gay and lesbian psychotherapy has grown dramatically over the last two decades. Indeed, there is an increasing number of professional journals and books, which makes staying current in any area of mental health a full-time job. Many clinicians can feel daunted by having to remain up-to-date in their subspecialty, as well as in the mental health field in general. In addition, there are many allied fields of medicine, sociology, biology, and gerontology which contribute to the richness and complexity. We are a heterogeneous community, mixed by gender, race, ethnicity, class, religion, and other demographics, each of which has special characteristics for us to know and understand. Being current and remaining current are two distinct and formidable tasks. This paper will focus upon how clinicians in private practice stay current in the field of research and practice knowledge while working in the gay and lesbian community. While hoping to provide some sources of information, this paper only begins to address some of the areas of research which affect our communities. *[Article copies available for a fee from The Haworth Document Delivery Service: 1-800-342-9678. E-mail address: getinfo@haworthpressinc.com]*

The title assigned to this paper seems to imply two things: that a clinician is able to be "current" at some point in time, and that a

---

Joel C. Frost, EdD, CGP, is an Associate in Psychology, Beth Israel Deaconess Medical Center, Boston; Instructor in Psychology, Harvard Medical School; Private Practice, Suite 214, 520 Commonwealth Avenue, Boston, MA 02215-2605.

[Haworth co-indexing entry note]: "Staying Current with Gay and Lesbian Research and Practice Knowledge." Frost, Joel C. Co-published simultaneously in *Journal of Gay & Lesbian Social Services* (The Haworth Press, Inc.) Vol. 8, No. 4, 1998, pp. 5-27; and: *Working with Gay Men and Lesbians in Private Psychotherapy Practice* (ed: Christopher J. Alexander) The Haworth Press, Inc., 1998, pp. 5-27. Single or multiple copies of this article are available for a fee from The Haworth Document Delivery Service [1-800-342-9678, 9:00 a.m. - 5:00 p.m. (EST). E-mail address: getinfo@haworthpressinc.com].

clinician can stay current with ongoing research and developments as a field matures. I believe both implications create difficulty for us all.

The field of gay and lesbian mental health has been growing and changing dramatically. There is a proliferation of books and articles on multiple aspects of gay and lesbian life. There is an ever-increasing number of out gay and lesbian clinicians advertising their services to the gay and lesbian community. In one Boston gay newspaper there are now 37 clinicians who advertise such services. One clinician even advertises "State-of-the-Art Psychotherapy." "State-of-the-Art" implies that one is on the cutting edge of new developments in a particular field.

Mental health with gays and lesbians has now become a specialty area to which some clinicians devote their entire clinical practice, while others have a blended practice of gays, lesbians, heterosexuals, and bisexuals. Yet, as our field expands as a specialty, staying current in any area of clinical research is more a hope than a reality, and in a blended practice one has to consider research from a plethora of clinical areas. Each clinician has to consider the developments relative to his/her theoretical orientation, clinical modality (individual, group, couple's, family psychotherapy), type of intervention (long-term, short-term, crisis-intervention), focus of intervention (psychotherapy, support, psychoeducation), general issues vs. special focus (e.g., eating disorders, trauma, substance usage), or type of population serviced (coming-out, aging gays or lesbians, adolescents, disabled). As we become more mainstream, we are increasingly faced with a daunting task of keeping informed even in our own field, as we broaden and deepen areas of expertise.

I have been in private practice for twelve years, and out of graduate school for fourteen years. My clinical training in graduate school was primarily psychoanalytic, and did not include courses in gay and lesbian theory, gay and lesbian development, or psychotherapy as applied to gays and lesbians. The only books on the topic were the traditional psychoanalytic texts which presented homosexuality only in pathological terms. It became a welcome relief to begin to find literature which was positive about homosexuality and homosexuals. Thus, my own base of knowledge has had to come from elsewhere, leaving me feeling that I never experienced a time when I was "current." In addition, I had to undo and re-work what little I was taught regarding homosexuality.

Graduate education has changed in that some universities do presently include courses on gay and lesbian theory and development, and do so in a positive manner. Therefore, as a large selection of practicing clinicians, we might be divided into those who had to undo, or make up for, what we were taught, or not taught, in graduate school, and those who have been relatively well provided for in their training. Those of us in the first group have had to rely upon alternative sources for our education and training.

What does it mean to stay current with gay and lesbian research? Indeed, in the twenty-four years since the American Psychiatric Association's 1973 official decision to discontinue labeling homosexuality as a diagnosis, there has been an ever-growing body of research and practice knowledge to review. In this paper, "research" will include data from research studies as well as theory, developmental work, and writings on various areas which affect psychotherapy with gay men and lesbian women.

In addition, there have been major shifts in our awareness of bisexuality. Historically, bisexuals have been seen by both the gay and lesbian community much the same way as by the heterosexual community—we were waiting for the bisexual to make up his or her mind and declare membership in one camp. It would seem that bisexuality has become a camp of its own, with a growing membership, and a growing body of research and literature (Buxton, 1994; D'Augelli & Patterson, 1995; Firestein, in press; Rotheram-Borus & Koopman, 1991; Weinberg, Williams, & Pryor, 1994).

I have written this paper from the point of view of a clinician in full-time private practice, who has little available time and resources to do the research required to remain continually "current." I have a hospital appointment where I supervise and teach group theory. This appointment in effect forces me to read. There is also some pressure to publish. The combination of these pressures actually helps me to stay as current as I can, knowing that there is always too much to read in too little time.

Some colleagues do find the time to read, while others do not. It seems that most gay and lesbian psychotherapists draw much of their practice knowledge from their own life experiences, a position which has been confirmed in informal conversations with other therapists. Most clinicians augment this practice knowledge with what they learn in their work with gay and lesbian clients.

A perennial issue has always been the question as to whether clinicians use research at all in their practices. Many clinicians seem to eschew participating in, or even reading, hard research following the completion of their doctoral dissertation. As the years pass since receiving our doctorate, we can begin to feel less familiar with how to read, evaluate, understand, and figure out how to apply research to our everyday clinical work. In the present state of mental health, many clinicians find themselves working more hours to make the same income. With increased pressure, many clinicians in private practice may find themselves becoming increasingly isolated, with less time and energy to devote to enhancing their research and practice knowledge. In talking with colleagues, most clinicians seem to rely upon conferences and workshops for this infusion of knowledge. However, this means that we must trust that those leading the workshops are staying current as they transmit the knowledge to us. As daunting as this task is, we all should consider that it is very important that we work to stay as current as possible as the field constantly changes and grows. This paper is an attempt to organize some information, and to point the reader in some directions.

I have broken this task down into a number of categories to provide an overview: General Approach, and Methods to Become and Remain "Current." In addition, I will address possible sources for clinicians: Internal and Personal, Internal to One's Clinical Practice, External Sources, Community Sources, and Miscellaneous Sources. Finally, I will include an area for Additional and Associated Research Areas. Even so, this will only be an attempt at broaching the subject; hopefully others will add to the process in additional articles.

GENERAL APPROACH

As psychotherapists, we help people change. As a group, we have witnessed a long history of mental health professionals devoted to changing more than was asked for by the gay or lesbian patient or client. Thus, as a professional group we may be more sensitive than other clinicians regarding what we will agree to attempt to change, and at whose request. It is not unusual for me to have clients initially entering psychotherapy request that I help them to alter their being gay, to help them become heterosexual. My response to them is based upon my understanding of the etiology of homosexuality, my role in the therapeutic relationship, my theoretical orientation, and the options that I can pose for their consideration. I also present that conversion therapies have not been found generally helpful over the lives of clients who have chosen that route. With all of this said, I am also aware that I have my own bias, which is in part based upon my own life choices.

In the clinical work with gays and lesbians, clarity of role relationship is a central starting point, as is theoretical orientation and an understanding of developmental theories. There continues to be much ongoing research regarding the possible biological, familial, environmental, and genetic "causes" of homosexuality. Whatever response that we have to the felt need for such research, and the lack of similar research zeal to find the "causes" of heterosexuality does not negate the fact that we all must have some stance as to etiology, even if our position is that we do not know (D'Augelli, 1994; Frost, in press; Isay, 1986a; Lewes, 1988; Stein, 1996).

Each clinician works within a framework of a theory base; however, there are many theories from which to choose. Freud and psychoanalytic theories, or Ego Psychology theories, help us to have an understanding of the development of internal structures. Mahler's work with children helps us to have some understanding of developmental needs and hierarchy (Mahler, Pine, & Bergman, 1975).

There are also developmental theories which are particular to gay and lesbian development. For anyone working with gays and lesbians, knowledge of these theories helps in understanding how gays and lesbians develop a positive gay or lesbian identity (Cass, 1996; Cass, 1979; Chan, 1989; Coleman, 1981/82; D'Augelli, 1994; D'Augelli & Patterson, 1995; DeMonteflores & Schultz, 1978; Groves & Ventura, 1983; Harry, 1993; Hencken & O'Dowd, 1977; Isay, 1986a; Isay, 1986b; Lewis, 1984; Minton & McDonald, 1983/84; Sophie, 1985/86; Troiden, 1989).

It is helpful to have a basic understanding of the theories of gay and lesbian relationships in terms of special characteristics which prohibit or assist their establishment, and factors which affect the longevity of relationships. We need to have an understanding of the role and prevalence of internalized homophobia, and how this is related to and different from the role and prevalence of internalized shame. There is a history of substance usage in our heterogeneous community, and clinicians must understand their own usage and stance regarding use. We practice in multiple modalities, each of which benefits patients and clients in different ways, sometimes in a complementary fashion. We need to consider when we offer individual, couple's, family, group, and conjoint modalities.

There is a trend within mental health to develop minimal practice criteria for clinicians to be recognized as sufficiently trained to work with particular populations. This process works most efficiently with some regulatory agency or organization being involved so as to help develop the criteria, and monitor training achievement. At this point, any clinician can specify that they are willing to work with gays and lesbians, or that they practice "gay affirmative" psychotherapy. The idea of establishing minimal practice criteria may seem more palatable if we think of applying them to non-gay and non-lesbian clinicians. However, how do we begin to think about this issue when considering that increasing numbers of clients are now selecting to work with clinicians based in some part on their open acknowledgment that they are gay or lesbian? In the short run, suffice it to say that we should all be aware that the field of gay and lesbian mental health is growing rapidly as a specialty, with an increasing amount that we might want to know.

METHODS TO BECOME AND REMAIN "CURRENT"

Overview Textbooks

One means of beginning with this task is to read comprehensive textbooks that provide an overview of historical perspectives and current research. We are fortunate to have such textbooks now being provided from within the gay and lesbian community. Robert P. Cabaj and Terry S. Stein (Cabaj & Stein, 1996) have produced a very complete overview which includes chapters on history, cross-cultural, multicultural, familial and genetic, biological, life cycle development, relationship patterning, substance abuse, psychotherapy, and training needs of new mental health professionals. This book is intended to be a textbook for graduate school training, although one significant topic area missing from this textbook is the use of support and/or psychotherapy groups with gays and lesbians.

Greenberg (1988) has provided a cross-cultural compilation of the social organization of homosexuality through history. In addition, there are texts which help us to put homosexuality into an historical, social, and cross-cultural perspective (Blumenfeld, 1992; Boswell, 1980; D'Augelli & Patterson, 1995; Garnets & Kimmel, 1993; Gonsiorek & Weinrich, 1991; Greene & Herek, 1994; Isay, 1996; Lewes, 1988; McWhirter, Sanders, & Reinisch, 1990; Miller, 1989; Weinberg, 1972). Alexander (1996) has brought together a unique collection of gay and lesbian clinicians writing on a wide range of research findings affecting many groups within the gay and lesbian community.

Professional Journals

There are dedicated journals which can keep us up-to-date: *Journal of Gay & Lesbian Psychotherapy,* The Haworth Medical Press; *Journal of Homosexuality,* The Haworth Press, Inc.; *Journal of Gay & Lesbian Social Services,* The Haworth Press, Inc.; and the new *Journal of the Gay and Lesbian Medical Association,* Plenum Publishing Corporation. In addition, there are periodic publications such as *Psychology & AIDS Exchange,* published by the American Psychological Association through the Office on AIDS Network. There are dedicated sections of major journals, such as the Summer Supplement, 1995, of the *Bulletin of the New York Academy of Medicine,* New York Academy of Medicine, which is subtitled "Perspectives in HIV Care: A View from the Front Lines."

Internal and Personal Sources

As broached above, I believe that it is fair to say that most all clinicians use their own life experiences as reference points in their clinical work. What may be different for gay and lesbian psychotherapists is the degree to which we rely upon our life experiences, and the gaps that we must negotiate in doing so. We do not have the luxury of beginning from the assumed position of "normalcy." Although society's acceptance of gays and lesbians has changed dramatically over the last few decades, gay and lesbian clinicians as a group represent internal snapshots from each stage of society's development. Coming out, and one's self-acceptance continues to be different for each new cohort of gays and lesbians, many of whom never come to our offices. We need to keep in perspective our internal scheme about being gay or lesbian as a function of our growing up when we did, and the internal scheme of the patient or client who developed when he or she did as we all try to adapt to the present set of societal conditions in the geographical location of our practice.

It may well be true that many or most clinicians use much of their own life experiences to inform them in their clinical work. Women may well understand women more quickly and intuitively, as may men with men. Clinicians who are parents may have an edge on understanding developmental stages as clients work through their issues. Continuing clinical experience with members of particular populations or clinical groups may provide opportunities for us to more deeply understand these populations. However, it may be a fallacy to think that the mere fact of being gay or lesbian is a sufficient basis to presume clinical knowledge or expertise in working with a gay or lesbian client.

In addition, clinicians often rely upon their own psychotherapy or psychoanalysis as a reference point. Clinicians often practice in a manner which is heavily influenced by their own psychotherapist. However, I believe that there is yet to be a cohort of gay and lesbian psychotherapists who have had their own psychotherapeutic experience(s) with an "out" gay or lesbian psychotherapist or psychoanalyst. I believe this to be a critically important consideration, and an important benchmark when attained. As a psychotherapy community within the larger gay and lesbian communities, I believe that we are still developing our understanding of the need for, and ways to, mentor each other. I believe that it would be helpful to have clinicians who are supervised by or are in psychotherapy with out gays and lesbians to write about these experiences. Such articles would lead us in the direction of research regarding the effects of sexual orientation on identity development, the degree to which there can be an amelioration of shame and internalized homophobia, the effects upon capacity for empathy, and the particulars of transference and countertransference when the sexual orientation of therapist and client are known and the same (as opposed to presumed sameness of heterosexuality).

Sources Internal to One's Practice

We learn and change as we practice. Thus the clients, supervisors, colleagues, and our own psychotherapists that we work with have a great influence upon us. I believe that we are also influenced by the modality in which we practice. There is an old saying that a client can only progress as far as a clinician will let him or her. Does the gay or lesbian clinician who only practices individual psychotherapy have the same perspective on what is possible for gay and lesbian clients as the clinician who also employs group, couple's, and/or family psychotherapy? When a gay or lesbian clinician does expand the modalities in which he or she works, it is essential for them to seek specialty training in that modality. In the past, this might be overlooked in that couple's, group, or family training organizations may not have had specialty tracks in working with gays and lesbians; this is no longer the case.

We are influenced by whether we have our clinical work supervised, and the level and quality of training and understanding of such supervisors. Do you work with a supervisor or supervisors, and are they gay, lesbian, bisexual, or heterosexual? Do you work in a peer supervision group, and do the same previous questions apply? Do the clinicians who are in supervision with you only practice in one modality? What we are exposed to continues to form and alter our working theories and framework. Do we only work with the same gender, only with gays or lesbians, or only one class, or one race?

External Sources

Many clinicians do not find that they have the time to read all that they should, and thus rely upon a seminal paper or book that they go back to periodically to renew a sense of a solid underpinning to their work.

Coming out	Management strategies for gays and lesbians in their job settings	Psychotherapy with gay men or lesbians
Cain, 1991	Griffin, 1992	Anthony, 1981/82
Cass, 1979	Murphy, 1992	Berger, 1983
DeMonteflores & Schultz, 1978	Troiden, 1979	Browning, Reynolds, & Dworkin, 1991
Hencken & O'Dowd, 1977	Woods & Harbeck, 1992	Buhrke & Douce, 1991

Coming out	Management strategies for gays and lesbians in their job settings	Psychotherapy with gay men or lesbians
Lewis, 1984	Cain, 1991	D'Augelli, 1994
Malyon, 1982	Morgan & Brown, 1991	Garnets, Hancock, Cochran, Goodchilds, & Peplau, 1991
Martin, 1991	Anthony, 1981/82	McCandlish, 1981/82
McDonald, 1982		Miranda & Storms, 1989
Sophie, 1985/86		Owen, 1986 Schwartz, 1989 Sobocinski, 1990 Stein, 1996 Tievsky, 1988

Group psychotherapy with gay men and lesbians	Gay/Lesbian adolescents	Theories of etiology
Conlin & Smith, 1981/82	Heron, 1983	Bailey, 1995
Frost, 1990	Martin, 1982	Burr, 1996
Frost, 1996	Sobocinski, 1990	Byne, 1993
Martin, 1982	Sullivan & Schneider, 1987	Money, 1993
Scwartz & Hartstein, 1986		Murphy, 1992

Richard Isay has been working for years to develop a body of clinical material from his work with gay men in New York (Isay, 1989; 1986a; 1986b; 1990). Many gay male clinicians refer to his work often.

A continuing dilemma with reading is that there are so many things to know, and so little time. Many clinicians who are gay or lesbian may have other specialties, so working with gay and lesbian clients may be a secondary or tertiary focus. Staying current in other areas of mental health may too often come first.

Mentors, peers, teachers, and conference speakers all make a significant impact upon our current understanding; conferences, workshops, and specialty training are important continuing sources of new and additional learning. For many of us, these venues augment what we may not have gotten in graduate training. These forums also offer the opportunity to teach, which is a wonderfully powerful way to stay current. Teaching forces us to make the time to read and research, and to organize the data into a form which is digestible to the audience.

Division 44 of the American Psychological Association (APA) is a rapidly growing group of psychologists who have developed such a large package of gay and lesbian programming at the annual APA Conference that clinicians can spend the entire time only attending gay and lesbian presentations. The Special Interest Group for Gay, Lesbian, and Bisexual Issues (SIGGLBI), a Special Interest Group of the American Group Psychotherapy Association (AGPA), has also grown in size and importance in that multi-disciplinary organization. SIGGLBI also sponsors much programming at the Annual AGPA Institute and Conference. Professional organizations provide peer learning and support, experiential and cognitive opportunities, as well as opportunities to teach and present your work.

What we are exposed to continually influences our understanding and our clinical work with patients and clients. It is incumbent on us to keep ourselves current by continuing to be open to new experiences. One such area is the developing bisexual community which now also has an annual conference.

Community Sources

Many of the larger metropolitan communities have gay and/or lesbian newspapers. While not a source of research, they provide a window into our communities, from the articles to the advertisements to the personal ads.

There is also a group of national gay and lesbian focused magazines, such as Genre, and OUT. The quality and level of the articles in these magazines may not be such that they qualify for research. However, when kept in the waiting room, patients and clients can find the short articles on relationships, dating, drug use, AIDS, the "circuit," sexual behavior, monogamy, or stereotypes provocative, which can generate reflection on their own behavior and ideas.

Miscellaneous Sources

We all have to have CEUs in order to maintain our licenses in mental health. There is a proliferation of opportunities for home study.

One company allows clinicians to do home study for CEUs in a series called *Directions in Clinical and Counseling Psychology!* Some of their offerings are gay, lesbian, or bisexual, although they may offer more if they received sufficient requests. Their address is: The Hatherleigh Company, 1114 First Avenue, Suite 500, New York, NY 10021.

I have also received a mailing for the 1997 *Guide to Behavioral Resources on the Internet,* at a cost of $245. Although this book seemed a bit expensive, it may well presage an increased usage of the Internet for mental health services as well as information. A less expensive ($19.95) resource book to find mental health resources is *The Insider's Guide to Mental Health Resources Online* (Grohol, 1997). The American Psychological Association has its own home page on the Web at www.apa.org.

ADDITIONAL AND ASSOCIATED PROFESSIONAL RESEARCH

HIV and AIDS

There is a constantly changing landscape regarding HIV and AIDS. Some overview sources which can assist are: *Psychology & AIDS Exchange,* published by the AIDS Resource Network of the Office on AIDS, American Psychological Association (202-336-6042). FOCUS is a monthly newsletter of the UCSF AIDS Health Project (415-476-6430).

There are many references regarding patient care and psychotherapy with gay men and lesbian women: Adib, Joseph, Ostrow, & James, 1991; Anastos & Palleja, 1991; Basen-Engquist, 1992; Beckett & Rutan, 1990; Crawford, Humfleet, Ribordy, Fung, & Vickers, 1991; Dilley, Pies, & Helquist, 1989; Fernandez & Levy, 1990; Field & Shore, 1992; Forstein, 1984; Frost, 1993; Frost, 1994; Georgianna & Johnston, 1993; Getzel & Mahoney, 1990; Gochros, 1992; Hays, Turner, & Coates, 1992; McGuire, Nieri, Abbott, Sheridan, & Fisher, 1995; Myers, 1992; Rotheram-Borus, Koopman, & Ehrhardt, 1991; Stuntzner-Gibson, 1991; Totten, Lamb, & Reeder, 1990; Tunnell, 1991; and Werth, 1992.

Caregivers undergo significant stress while working with clients infected with HIV, or who have AIDS. There are many articles and research findings which help us to understand these stresses and what to do about them: Adams, 1991; Frost, 1994; Grossman and Silverstein, 1993; McKusick, 1988; Nashman, Hoare, and Heddesheimer, 1990; Oktay, 1992; Pearlin, Semple, and Turner, 1988; Piemme and Bolle, 1990; Silverman, 1993; and Simon, 1988.

LESBIAN AND GAY COUPLES

Often, there is a tendency to use one's own primary relationship as a central tool for understanding gay or lesbian couple's development and struggles. There are distinct advantages and disadvantages to the exclusive use of our own experiences as a template for relationships. Thankfully, there is a developing body of research specific to gay and lesbian couples.

There are many creative ways in which gay men and lesbians form couples, many of which are not traditional. The definition of "couple" has needed to be expanded as more gay men and lesbians have children and establish family units. As with most areas in society, research remains behind the cutting edge. However, there are some places to begin (Berger, 1990; Burch, 1990; Carl, 1990; Clunis & Green, 1988; Falco, 1991; McCandlish, 1981/82; McWhirter & Mattison, 1984). Gay and lesbian parents are also increasing in numbers (Barret & Robinson, 1990; Bozett, 1987; Laird & Green, 1996).

AGING

As a new cohort of "Baby Boomer" ages and gays and lesbians enter their 50s, there is a growing literature on gay and lesbian aging (Adelman, Berger, Boyd, Doublex, Freedman, Hubbard et al., 1993; Adelman, 1991; Berger, 1982a; Berger, 1982b; Berger, 1993; Berger & Kelly, 1986; Friend, 1991; Friend, 1987; Frost, in press; Healy, 1994; Kimmel, 1978; Shannon & Woods, 1991). Although already outdated, Hubbard (1993) is a rich source of organizations, articles, books, research, and essays on gay and lesbian aging.

Baby boomers now make up one third of the population of the United States, which means that there is a large number of gays and lesbians 50 and over. As this cohort moves into their later years, we need to develop better research on normative gay aging, intervention strategies, housing and financial suggestions and options, cooperative and creative living arrangements, preferences for blended or dedicated nursing homes for gays and lesbians, and the particular concerns of the aged. It is up to us to do this research as well as to read what has been written. Indeed, in the next few years gay/lesbian-geropsychology may well become a subspecialty within the specialty of gay and lesbian mental health.

HOMOPHOBIA AND SHAME

We have had many articles and books which look at the effects of homophobia on the gay and lesbian communities (Blumenfeld, 1992; D'Augelli, 1989; DeCrescenzo, 1984; Douglas, Kalman, & Kalman, 1985; Forstein, 1984; Garfinkle & Morin, 1978; Graham, Rawlings, Halpern, & Hermes, 1984; Malyon, 1981/82; McGuire et al., 1995; Messing, Schoenberg, & Stephens, 1984; Neisen, 1990; Randall, 1989; Royse & Birge, 1987; Tievsky, 1988; Triplet & Sugarman, 1987; Whitam, 1991; Young, Henderson, & Marx, 1990). In addition, there is a growing attention to the effect of shame on gay and lesbian development (Kaufman & Raphael, 1996; Lewis, 1987).

THEORETICAL ORIENTATION

There is often a moment of discomfort when one is asked: "What is your theoretical orientation?" There are many reasons for this discomfort. A clinician can feel that in order to declare his or her theoretical orientation means that he or she had better be an expert in that area; often the response "eclectic" lessens some anxiety. Given many years of persecution at the hands of the psychoanalytic community, clinicians may hesitate to declare that they are psychoanalytically oriented, or at least psychodynamically. However, for those of us who were trained in that theoretical orientation, there are new books which present a refreshing use of psychoanalytic theory in working with gays and lesbians (Domenici & Lesser, 1995; Isay, 1990; Lewes, 1988; Mitchell, 1981; Rutkin, 1995).

PRACTICE DEMOGRAPHICS

Psychotherapy with gay men and lesbian women has become a specialty practice. Many clinicians have exclusively gay, lesbian, or mixed gay and lesbian practices. I have never heard of any research, or even of a question regarding the need for research, into the phenomena of heterosexual psychotherapists having a practice which is exclusively heterosexual. The same could be said for a clinician limiting his or her practice along religious, racial, ethnic, or symptom criteria. As we become increasingly a presence in the field of mental health, I presume that there will be questions as to the effects of the demographics of our practices. My bias is that there are benefits and drawbacks to having a narrow focused practice. There may be a need to look more closely into the belief that those of us who are gay or lesbian presume we know best how to work with gay and lesbian clients. Indeed, there may be an expanding arena for research within the modalities and demographics of our own practices as we become more professionally organized. I would think that it would behoove us to initiate such research ourselves rather than become the subjects of the research of others. As stated earlier, we may want to begin addressing the issue of minimal practice standards and criteria, rather than have them developed from outside of the community.

CONCLUSIONS AND RECOMMENDATIONS

This paper is in no means considered by this author to be sufficient in addressing the scope of topics, or the research citations necessary to have an overview of current research with gay men and lesbian women. In even beginning this paper it became clear that I do not know what "current" would even mean. In this regard, as a psychologist in private practice, I believe that my state of frustration and intimidation is probably not that much different than many other clinicians in private practice trying to stay knowledgeable as we work with our gay and lesbian clients.

I find that in the end, I rely upon my own life experience, the experiences of the clients that I work with, what I learn by regularly attending workshops and conferences, and a few key articles and books to keep me relatively confidant that I know what I am doing.

Many colleagues have told me that they feel the same about their work as well.

For every topic that I have included here, there are as many that I have not included. A paper cannot be long enough to begin to cover the additional needs regarding research in the areas of breast and uterine cancer that affect lesbians in our community, gay and lesbian teenage development, substance usage, the abuse literature, or legal, financial, or political findings that increasingly affect our heterogeneous community as more gays and lesbians have children and form family units.

I hope that each of us realizes that it is important to write and publish as a continuing contribution to the growing body of research and literature on gays and lesbians. It is up to us to remain as current as possible as our field develops, so that we are delivering the best care possible to those who depend upon us. It is also important that we continue to contribute to the growing body of research, as we are an abundantly rich and heterogeneous collection of individuals.

REFERENCES

Adams, J. (June 10, 1991). Grief, stress, loss–all weigh heavily on AIDS workers. *The Boston Globe*, pp. 35-37.

Adelman, J., Berger, R., Boyd, M., Doublex, V., Freedman, M., Hubbard, W. S., Kight, M., Kochman, A., Meyer, M. K. R., & Raphael, S. M. (1993). *Lambda gray: A practical, emotional, and spiritual guide for gays and lesbians who are growing older.* North Hollywood, CA: Newcastle Publishing.

Adelman, M. (1991). Stigma, gay lifestyles, and adjustment to aging: A study of later-life gay men and lesbians. In J. A. Lee (Ed.), *Gay mid-life and maturity* (pp. 7-32). New York: The Haworth Press, Inc.

Adib, S. M., Joseph, J. G., Ostrow, D. G., & James, S. A. (1991). Predictors of relapse in sexual practices among homosexual men. *AIDS Education and Prevention, 3*(4), 293-304.

Alexander, C. J. (Ed.). (1996). *Gay and lesbian mental health: A sourcebook for practitioners.* New York: Harrington Park Press.

Anastos, K., & Palleja, S. M. (1991). Caring for women at risk of HIV infection. *Journal of General Internal Medicine, 6*(Jan/Feb Supplement), S40-S46.

Anthony, B. D. (1981/82). Lesbian client–lesbian therapist: Opportunities and challenges in working together. *Journal of Homosexuality, 7*(2/3), 45-57.

Bailey, J. M. (1995). Biological perspectives on sexual orientation. In A.R. D'Augelli & C.J. Patterson (Eds.), *Lesbian, gay and bisexual identities over the lifespan,* pp. 102-135. New York: Oxford University Press.

Barret, R., & Robinson, B. (1990). *Gay fathers.* New York: McMillan.

Basen-Engquist, K. (1992). Psychosocial predictors of "safer sex" behaviors in young adults. *AIDS Education and Prevention, 4*(2), 120-134.

Beckett, A., & Rutan, J. S. (1990). Treating persons with ARC and AIDS in group psychotherapy. *International Journal of Group Psychotherapy, 40*(1), 19-29.

Berger, R. (1983). What is a homosexual: A definitive model. *Social Work, 28,* 132-141.

Berger, R. (1990). Men together: Understanding the gay couple. *Journal of Homosexuality, 19*(3), 31-49.

Berger, R. M. (1982a). *Gay & gray: The older homosexual man.* Boston: Alyson Publications, Inc.

Berger, R. M. (1982b). The unseen minority: Older gays and lesbians. *Social Work, 27*(3), 236-242.

Berger, R. M. (1993). How I found my way home: Confessions of an older gay man. In J. Adelman et al., *Lambda gray: A practical, emotional, and spiritual guide for gays and lesbians who are growing older* (pp. 17-31). North Hollywood, CA: Newcastle Publishing.

Berger, R. M., & Kelly, J. J. (1986). Working with homosexuals of the older population. *Social Casework, 67*(4), 203-210.

Blumenfeld, W. J. (1992). *Homophobia: How we all pay the price.* Boston: Beacon Press.

Bozett, F. (1987). *Gay and lesbian parents.* Westport, Connecticut: Praeger.

Browning, C., Reynolds, A. L., & Dworkin, S. H. (1991). Affirmative psychotherapy for lesbian women. *The Counseling Psychologist, 19*(2), 177-196.

Buhrke, R. A., & Douce, L. A. (1991). Training issues for counseling psychologists in working with lesbian women and gay men. *The Counseling Psychologist, 19*(2), 216-234.

Burch, B. (1990). *On intimate terms: The psychology of difference in lesbian relationships.* Chicago: University of Illinois Press.

Burr, C. (1996). *A separate creation: The search for the biological origins of sexual orientation.* New York: Hyperion.

Byne, W., & Parsons, B. (1993). Human sexual orientation: The biological theories reappraised. *Archives of General Psychiatry, 50,* 228-239.

Cabaj, R. P., & Stein, T. S. (Eds.). (1996). *Textbook of homosexuality and mental health.* Washington, D.C.: American Psychiatric Press, Inc.

Cain, R. (1991). Stigma management and gay identity development. *Social Work, 36*(1), 67-73.

Carl, D. (1990). *Counseling same-sex couples.* New York: Norton.

Cass, V. (1996). Sexual orientation identity formation: A western phenomenon. In R. P. Cabaj & T. S. Stein (Eds.), *Textbook of homosexuality and mental health* (pp. 227-251). Washington, D.C.: American Psychiatric Press, Inc.

Cass, V. C. (1979). Homosexual identity formation: A theoretical model. *Journal of Homosexuality, 4,* 219-235.

Chan, C. S. (1989). Issues of identity development among Asian-American lesbians and gay men. *Journal of Counseling and Development, 68,* 16-20.

Clunis, D., & Green, G. (1988). *Lesbian couples.* Seattle, WA: The Seal Press.

Coleman, E. (1981/82). Developmental stages of the coming out process. *Journal of Homosexuality, 7,* 31-43.

Conlin, D., & Smith, J. (1981/82). Group psychotherapy for gay men. *Journal of Homosexuality, 7*(2/3), 105-112.

Crawford, I., Humfleet, G., Ribordy, S. C., Fung, H. C., & Vickers, V. L. (1991). Stigmatization of AIDS patients by mental health professionals. *Professional Psychology: Research and Practice, 22*(5), 357-361.

D'Augelli, A. (1994). Lesbian and gay male development. In B. Greene & G. M. Herek (Eds.), *Lesbian and gay psychology: Theory, research, and clinical application* (pp. 118-132). Thousand Oaks, CA: Sage.

D'Augelli, A. R. (1989). AIDS fears and homophobia among rural nursing personnel. *AIDS Education and Prevention, 1*(4), 277-284.

D'Augelli, A. R., & Patterson, C. J. (Ed.). (1995). *Lesbian, gay, and bisexual identities over the lifespan: Psychological perspectives.* New York: Oxford University Press.

DeCrescenzo, T. A. (1984). Homophobia: A study of the attitudes of mental health professionals toward homosexuality. *Journal of Social Work & Human Sexuality, 2,* 115-136.

DeMonteflores, C., & Schultz, S. J. (1978). Coming out: Similarities and differences for lesbians and gay men. *Journal of Social Issues, 34,* 59-72.

Dilley, J. W., Pies, C., & Helquist, M. (1989). *Face to face: A guide to AIDS counseling.* San Francisco: University of California.

Domenici, T., & Lesser, R. C. (Eds.). (1995). *Disorienting sexuality: Psychoanalytic reappraisals of sexual identities.* New York: Routledge.

Douglas, C. J., Kalman, C. M., & Kalman, T. F. (1985). Homophobia among physicians and nurses: An empirical study. *Hospital & Community Psychiatry, 36*(12), 1309-1311.

Falco, K. (1991). *Psychotherapy with lesbian clients.* New York: Brunner/Mazel.

Fassinger, R. E. (1991). The hidden minority: Issues and challenges in working with lesbian women and gay men. *The Counseling Psychologist, 19*(2), 157-176.

Fernandez, F., & Levy, J. K. (1990). Diagnosis and management of HIV primary dementia. In D. G. Ostrow (Eds.), *Behavioral Aspects of AIDS* (pp. 235-247). New York: Plenum.

Field, H. L., & Shore, M. (1992). Living and dying with AIDS: Report of a three-year psychotherapy group. *GROUP, 16*(3), 156-164.

Forstein, M. (1984). The psychosocial impact of the acquired immunodeficiency syndrome. *Seminars in Oncology, 11*(1), 77-82.

Friend, J. A. (1991). Older lesbians and gay people: A theory of successful aging. In J. A. Lee (Ed.), *Gay mid-life and maturity* (pp. 99-118). New York: The Haworth Press, Inc.

Friend, R. A. (1987). The individual and social psychology of aging: Clinical implications for lesbians and gay men. *Journal of Homosexuality, 14*(1/2), 307-331.

Frost, J. (1994). Support groups for medical caregivers of people with HIV diseases. *Group, 18*(3), 141-153.

Frost, J. C. (1990). A developmentally keyed scheme for the placement of gay men into psychotherapy groups. *International Journal of Group Psychotherapy, 42*(2), 155-167.

Frost, J. C. (1993). Group psychotherapy with HIV-positive and AIDS patients. In A. Alonso & H. I. Swiller (Eds.), *Group therapy in clinical practice* (pp. 255-270). Washington, DC: American Psychiatric Press, Inc.

Frost, J. C. (1994). Taking a sexual history with gay patients in psychotherapy. In S. A. Cadwell, R. A. Burnham, & M. Forstein (Eds.), *Therapists on the front line: Psychotherapy with gay men in the age of AIDS* (pp. 163-183). Washington, DC: American Psychiatric Press, Inc.

Frost, J. C. (1996). Working with gay men in psychotherapy groups. In M. P. Andronico (Eds.), *Men in groups: Insights, interventions, and psychoeducational work* (pp. 163-179). Washington, DC: American Psychological Association.

Frost, J. C. (in press). Group psychotherapy with the aging gay male: What constitutes older? *Group*.

Frost, J.C. (in press). Countertransference considerations for the gay male when leading psychotherapy groups for gay men. *International Journal for Group Psychotherapy*.

Garfinkle, E. M., & Morin, S. F. (1978). Psychologists' attitudes toward homosexual psychotherapy clients. *Journal of Social Issues, 34*, 101-112.

Garnets, L., Hancock, K. A., Cochran, S. D., Goodchilds, J., & Peplau, L. A. (1991). Issues in psychotherapy with lesbians and gay men. A survey of psychologists. *American Psychologist, 46*(9), 964-972.

Garnets, I. D., & Kimmel, D. C. (Eds.) (1993). *Psychological perspectives on lesbian & gay male experience*. New York: Columbia University Press.

Georgianna, C., & Johnston, M. W. (1993). Duty to protect: The gay community response. *FOCUS: A Guide to AIDS Research and Counseling*, pp. 1-4.

Getzel, G. S., & Mahoney, K. F. (1990). Confronting human finitude: Group work with people with AIDS (PWAs). *Journal of Gay & Lesbian Psychotherapy, 1*(3), 105-119.

Gochros, H. L. (1992). The sexuality of gay men with HIV infection. *Social Work, 37*(2), 105-109.

Graham, D. L., Rawlings, E. I., Halpern, H. S., & Hermes, J. (1984). Therapists' needs for training in counseling lesbians and gay men. *Professional Psychology: Research and Practice, 15*, 482-496.

Greenberg, D. F. (1988). *The construction of homosexuality*. Chicago: The University of Chicago Press.

Griffin, P. (1992). From hiding out to coming out: Empowering lesbian and gay educators. *Journal of Homosexuality*, 167-196.

Grohol, J. M. (1997). *The insider's guide to mental health resources online*. New York: Guilford Publications, Inc.

Grossman, A., & Silverstein, C. (1993). Facilitating support groups for professionals working with people with AIDS. *Social Work, 38*(2), 144-151.

Groves, P., & Ventura, L. (1983). The lesbian coming out process: Therapeutic considerations. *The Personnel and Guidance Journal* (November), 146-149.

Harry, J. (1993). Being out: A general model. *Journal of Homosexuality, 26*(1), 25-39.

Hays, R. B., Turner, H., & Coates, T. J. (1992). Social support, AIDS-related symptoms, and depression among gay men. *Journal of Consulting and Clinical Psychology, 60*(3), 463-469.

Healy, S. (1994). Diversity with a difference: On being old and lesbian. *Journal of Gay & Lesbian Social Services, 1*(1), 109-117.

Hencken, J. D., & O'Dowd, W. T. (1977). Coming out as an aspect of identity formation. *Gai Saber, 1*, 18-22.

Heron, A. (Ed.). (1983). *One teenager in ten: Writings by gay and lesbian youth.* Boston: Alyson.

Hubbard, W. S. (1993). Resources. In J. Adelman, R. Berger, M. Boyd, V. Doublex, M. Freedman, W. S. Hubbard, M. Kight, A. Kochman, M. K. R. Meyer, & S.M. Raphael (Eds.), *Lambda gray: A practical, emotional, and spiritual guide for gays and lesbians who are growing older* (pp. 133-179). North Hollywood, CA: New-castle Publishing.

Isay, R. (1989). *Being homosexual: Gay men and their development.* New York: Farrar, Straus, & Giroux.

Isay, R. A. (1986a). The development of sexual identity in homosexual men. In *The psychoanalytic study of the child* (pp. 467-489). New Haven, CT: Yale University Press.

Isay, R. A. (1986b). Homosexuality in homosexual and heterosexual men: Some distinctions and implications for treatment. In G. I. Fogel, F. M. Lane, & R. S. Liebert (Eds.), *The psychology of men* (pp. 277-299). New York: Basic Books.

Isay, R. A. (1990). Psychoanalytic theory and the therapy of gay men. In McWhirter, Sanders, & Reinisch (Eds.), *Homosexuality/Heterosexuality* (pp. 283-303). New York: Oxford Universities Press.

Isay, R. A. (1996). *Becoming gay: The journey to self-acceptance.* New York: Pantheon.

Kaufman, G., & Raphael, L. (1996). *Coming out of shame.* New York: Doubleday.

Kimmel, D. C. (1978). Adult development and aging: A gay perspective. *Journal of Social Issues, 34*(3), 113-130.

Laird, J., & Green, R. J. (1996). *Lesbians and gays in couples and families: A handbook for therapists.* San Francisco: Jossey-Bass, Publishers.

Lewes, K. (1988). *The psychoanalytic theory of male homosexuality.* New York: Simon and Schuster.

Lewis, H. B. (Ed.). (1987). *The role of shame in symptom formation.* Hillsdale, NJ: Lawrence Erlbaum Associates.

Lewis, L. (1984). The coming out process for lesbians: Integrating a stable identity. *Social Work* (Sept/Oct), 464-469.

Mahler, M. S., Pine, F., & Bergman, A. (1975). *The psychological birth of the human infant.* New York: Basic Books.

Malyon, A. (1981/82). Psychotherapeutic implications of internalized homophobia in gay men. *Journal of Homosexuality, 7*, 59-69.

Malyon, A. K. (1982). Biphasic aspects of homosexual identity formation. *Psychotherapy: Theory, Research and Practice, 19*(3), 335-340.

Martin, A. (1982). Some issues in the treatment of gay and lesbian patients. *Psychotherapy: Theory, Research and Practice, 19*(3), 341-348.

Martin, A. D. (1982). Learning to hide: The socialization of the gay adolescent. In S.C. Feinstein, J.G. Looney, A.Z. Schwartzberg, & A.D. Sorosky (Eds.), *Adolescent psychiatry: Development and clinical studies, 10* (pp. 52-65). Chicago: University of Chicago.

Martin, H. P. (1991). The coming-out process for homosexuals. *Hospital and Community Psychiatry, 42*, 158-162.

McCandlish, B. M. (1981/82). Therapeutic issues with lesbian couples. *Journal of Homosexuality, 7*(2/3), 71-78.

McDonald, G. J. (1982). Individual differences in the coming out process for gay men: Implications for theoretical models. *Journal of Homosexuality, 8*, 47-60.

McGuire, J., Nieri, D., Abbott, D., Sheridan, K., & Fisher, R. (1995). Do Tarasoff principles apply in AIDS-related psychotherapy? Ethical decision making and the role of therapist homophobia and perceived client dangerousness. *Professional Psychology: Research and Practice, 26*(6), 608-611.

McKusick, L. (1988). The impact of AIDS on practitioner and client: Notes for the therapeutic relationship. *American Psychologist, 43*(11), 935-940.

McWhirter, D., & Mattison, A. (1984). *The male couple.* Englewood Cliffs, New Jersey: Prentice-Hall.

Messing, A. E., Schoenberg, R., & Stephens, R. K. (1984). Confronting homophobia in health care settings: Guidelines for social work practice. *Journal of Social Work & Human Sexuality, 2*, 65-74.

Minton, H. L., & McDonald, G. J. (1983/84). Homosexual identity formation as a developmental process. *Journal of Homosexuality, 9*(2/3), 91-104.

Miranda, J., & Storms, M. (1989). Psychological adjustment of lesbians and gay men. *Journal of Counseling and Development, 68*, 41-45.

Mitchell, S. A. (1981). The psychoanalytic treatment of homosexuality: Some technical considerations. *International Review of Psycho-Analysis, 8*, 63-80.

Money, J. (1993). Sin, sickness, or status? Homosexual gender identity and psychoneuroendicrinology. In Garnets, L.D. & Kimmel, D.C. (Eds.) *Psychological perspectives on lesbian and gay male experience.* New York: Columbia University Press.

Morgan, K. S., & Brown, L. S. (1991). Lesbian career development, work behavior, and vocational counseling. *The Counseling Psychologist, 19*(2), 273-291.

Murphy, B. C. (1992). Educating mental health professionals about gay and lesbian issues. *Journal of Homosexuality*, 229-246.

Myers, M. T. (1992). The African-American experience with HIV disease. *Focus: A Guide to AIDS Research and Counseling, 7*(4), 1-4.

Nashman, H. W., Hoare, C. H., & Heddesheimer, J. C. (1990). Stress and satisfaction among professionals who care for AIDS patients. *Hospital Topics, 68*(1), 22-28.

Neisen, J. H. (1990). Heterosexism: Redefining homophobia for the 1990s. *Journal of Gay & Lesbian Psychotherapy, 1*(3), 21-35.

Oktay, J. S. (1992). Burnout in hospital social workers who work with AIDS patients. *Social Work, 37*(5), 432-439.

Owen, W. F. (1986). The clinical approach to the male homosexual patient. *Medical Clinics of North America, 70*(3), 499-535.

Pearlin, L. I., Semple, S., & Turner, H. (1988). Stress of AIDS caregiving: A preliminary overview of the issues. *Death Studies, 12*(5-6), 1-17.

Piemme, J. A., & Bolle, J. L. (1990). Coping with grief in response to caring for persons with AIDS. *American Journal of Occupational Therapy, 44*(3), 266-269.

Randall, C. E. (1989). Lesbian phobia among BSN educators: A survey. *Journal of Nursing Education, 28*(7), 302-306.

Rotheram-Borus, M. J., Koopman, C., & Ehrhardt, A. A. (1991). Homeless youths and HIV infection. *American Psychologist, 46*(11), 1188-1197.

Royse, D., & Birge, B. (1987). Homophobia and attitudes towards AIDS patients among medical, nursing, and paramedical students. *Psychological Reports, 61*, 867-870.

Rutkin, R. (1995). Psychoanalysis with gay and lesbian people: An interpersonal perspective. In T. Domenici & R. C. Lesser (Eds.), *Disorienting sexuality* (pp. 177-185). New York: Routledge.

Schwartz, R. D. (1989). When the therapist is gay: Personal and clinical reflections. *Journal of Gay & Lesbian Psychotherapy, 1*(1), 41-51.

Scwartz, R. D., & Hartstein, N. B. (1986). Group psychotherapy with gay men: Theoretical and clinical considerations. In T. S. Stein & C. J. Cohen (Eds.), *Contemporary perspectives on psychotherapy with lesbians and gay men* (pp. 157-177). New York: Plenum.

Shannon, J., & Woods, W. (1991). Affirmative psychotherapy for gay men. *The Counseling Psychologist, 19*(2), 197-215.

Silverman, D. (1993). Psychosocial impact of HIV-related caregiving on health providers: A review and recommendations for the role of psychiatry. *American Journal of Psychiatry, 150*(5), 1-8.

Simon, R. (1988). Special Issue: Confronting the specter of AIDS: What do therapists have to offer? *The Family Networker, 12*(1), 20-51.

Sobocinski, M. R. (1990). Ethical principles in the counseling of gay and lesbian adolescents: Issues of autonomy, competence, and confidentiality. *Professional Psychology: Research and Practice, 21*(4), 240-247.

Sophie, J. (1985/86). A critical examination of stage theories of lesbian identity development. *Journal of Homosexuality, 12*(2), 39-51.

Stein, T. S. (1996). A critique of approaches to changing sexual orientation. In R. P. Cabaj & T. S. Stein (Eds.), *Textbook of homosexuality and mental health* (pp. 525-537). Washington, D.C.: American Psychiatric Press, Inc.

Stuntzner-Gibson, D. (1991). Women and HIV disease: An emerging social crisis. *Social Work, 36*(1), 22-28.

Sullivan, T., & Schneider, M. (1987). Development and identity issues with adolescent homosexuality. *Child and Adolescent Social Work, 4*, 13-24.

Tievsky, D. L. (1988). Homosexual clients and homophobic social workers. *Journal of Independent Social Work, 2*, 51-62.

Totten, G., Lamb, D. H., & Reeder, G. D. (1990). *Tarasoff* and confidentiality in AIDS-related psychotherapy. *Professional Psychology: Research and Practice, 21*(3), 155-160.

Triplet, R. G., & Sugarman, D. B. (1987). Reactions to AIDS victims: Ambiguity breeds contempt. *Personality and Social Psychology Bulletin, 13*(2), 265-274.

Troiden, R. R. (1979). Becoming homosexual: A model for gay identity acquisition. *Psychiatry, 42*, 362-373.

Troiden, R. R. (1989). The formation of homosexual identities. *Journal of Homosexuality, 17*(1/2), 43-73.

Tunnell, G. (1991). Complications in group psychotherapy with AIDS patients. *International Journal of Group Psychotherapy, 41*(4), 481-498.

Werth, J. L. (1992). Rational suicide and AIDS: Considerations for the psychotherapist. *The Counseling Psychologist, 20*(4), 645-659.

Whitam, F. L. (1991). From sociology: Homophobia and heterosexism in sociology. *Journal of Gay & Lesbian Psychotherapy, 1*(4), 31-44.

Woods, S. E., & Harbeck, K. M. (1992). Living in two worlds: The identity management strategies used by lesbian physical educators. *Journal of Homosexuality,* 141-166.

Young, M., Henderson, M. M., & Marx, D. (1990). Attitudes of nursing students towards patients with AIDS. *Psychological Reports, 67*(2), 491-497.

The Business of Private Practice:
Marketing Strategies
for Gay and Lesbian Therapists

Christopher J. Alexander

SUMMARY. To have a successful private practice, clinicians must see themselves as both helpers and entrepreneurs. Yet, many clinicians are reluctant to view their practices as businesses that need to be marketed to consumers of mental health services. Without effective marketing and business planning, private practitioners face difficulty in establishing and maintaining a viable practice. This chapter covers basic strategies gay and lesbian therapists can utilize to effectively market and promote their services to the community. *[Article copies available for a fee from The Haworth Document Delivery Service: 1-800-342-9678. E-mail address: getinfo@haworthpressinc.com]*

BACKGROUND

For many counselors, psychologists and social workers, having a private psychotherapy practice is a desired professional goal. Private practice affords clinicians the independence and autonomy often not associated with more traditional forms of employment. Also, since private practitioners can determine how many hours a week they see clients, there is often ample opportunity to simultaneously pursue other professional endeavors such as research, teaching, writing, or working in an agency or clinic.

Christopher J. Alexander, PhD, is a licensed clinical psychologist in Santa Fe, NM. He can be reached at 620-B W. San Francisco Street, Santa Fe, NM 87501.

[Haworth co-indexing entry note]: "The Business of Private Practice: Marketing Strategies for Gay and Lesbian Therapists." Alexander, Christopher J. Co-published simultaneously in *Journal of Gay & Lesbian Social Services* (The Haworth Press, Inc.) Vol. 8, No. 4, 1998, pp. 29-42; and: *Working with Gay Men and Lesbians in Private Psychotherapy Practice* (ed: Christopher J. Alexander) The Haworth Press, Inc., 1998, pp. 29-42. Single or multiple copies of this article are available for a fee from The Haworth Document Delivery Service [1-800-342-9678, 9:00 a.m. - 5:00 p.m. (EST). E-mail address: getinfo@haworthpressinc.com].

What becomes disconcerting for many clinicians, however, is that few graduate counseling or psychology programs provide guidance or advice on how to successfully develop and promote a private practice. In turn, clinicians may invest the time and expense of establishing a private practice, only to find that their dreams of having a steady flow of clients do not come true. It is not uncommon for licensed clinicians to share with colleagues at meetings, consultation groups, or workshops that maintaining a private practice is more challenging than they ever realized. Often, there is resentment expressed that they were not forewarned of this reality.

When managed care became a dominant force in the field of mental health, clinicians had various opinions about what effect it would have on the private practitioner. Some felt that the referrals managed care companies could provide would be a welcome adjunct to other ways in which they obtained clients. Others believed that managed care would result in the end of independent practice. Though some private psychotherapy practices have been negatively affected because of managed care, many others are doing quite well.

Those private practitioners who are doing well without relying upon managed care referrals have learned that they must find other ways of generating clients. By utilizing effective advertising and marketing strategies, these clinicians are finding ways of maintaining professional integrity while several of their colleagues feel held hostage to the managed care industry.

Collectively, it is safe to conclude that there has been much concern expressed by many health care professionals, not just in mental health, about managed care. Resentment over the ways in which diagnostic and therapeutic methods are questioned by managed care companies has caused quite a stir in the health care world.

Even though professional associations such as the American Psychological Association and the American Medical Association publicly accuse managed care companies of over-regulating the health care field, the reality is that a significant percentage of Americans who receive work-place insurance have some form of managed care coverage. This means that–at least for now–health care professionals must find ways of accommodating the reality of managed health care, while at the same time adhering to personal and professional ethics around psychological and medical treatment (Adams, 1987).

Consumers, on the other hand, are not necessarily paying as much attention to managed care as are health professionals. Rather, many realize that there may come a time when they need psychological or medical services, and at that time they begin the search to see what is available in terms of help.

Use of Psychotherapy by Gays and Lesbians

There is little current data available on what percentage of gay men and lesbians utilize psychological services. Of the studies published to date, however (Bradford & Ryan, 1987; Cardea, 1985; Hoagland, 1988; Morgan, 1992; Rudolph, 1988), most indicate that lesbians are more likely to seek out the services of a mental health professional than are gay men. Estimates of psychotherapy use by gay men range from 25 to 65% (Rudolph, 1988), whereas the percentages for lesbians may be as high as 75%.

In one of the earlier studies on this topic, Modrcin and Wyers (1990) studied 78 lesbian and 50 gay male couples to determine the ways in which couples seek help for relationship problems. These researchers found that 39% of the sample had utilized professional help in the past to help solve relationship problems, with lesbian couples using psychological services more than gay male couples. The authors conclude that gay male couples appear to be reluctant to seek professional help for their relationship problems, perhaps because men find it difficult admitting to needing help.

In a more recent study on the health care needs of lesbians (Bradford, Ryan, & Rothblum, 1994), researchers surveyed 1,925 lesbians from all 50 U.S. states. These researchers found that 73% of the women surveyed were in counseling or had received some form of mental health support from a professional mental health counselor at some time in the past. The authors note that this figure stands in striking contrast to the 13.8% national base rate of mental health service usage by adult women.

The reasons cited by this sample for going to therapy were because of sadness or depression (50%), relationship difficulties (44%), problems with family (34%), and problems with friends (10%). The majority of the sample who had been in counseling had done so for one year or less.

These studies, taken together with anecdotal evidence, indicate that there is a need for psychological services by large numbers of gay men and lesbians. This suggests that gay and lesbian psychotherapists wanting to work with sexual minorities have ample opportunity, as long as they can effectively market their practice to these men and women.

THE BUSINESS OF PRIVATE PRACTICE

One truth affecting all mental health professionals who want to sustain a private practice is that, in addition to offering a service–psychotherapy–they are also operating a business. As Beigel and Earle (1990) note, however, many psychotherapists were drawn to the field of mental health by a desire to help people, particularly those without much support or resource in their lives. Since the business, or corporate, world has often been perceived as self-serving and at times, exploitative, there has been a natural reluctance on the part of psychotherapists to view themselves as part of the business community.

These perspectives have made it difficult for some mental health professionals to think of their work from a business perspective, where terms such as goals, services offered, profitability, and competition are common. The effect of this is that these subjects have been treated by many psychotherapists as taboo, particularly as they pertain to finances.

Other health care professions, on the other hand, have had less of a problem integrating these terms and concepts into their practices. For example, it is not difficult to find out the average cost of service or yearly salary of physicians, dentists or veterinarians in many communities. But how many psychotherapists are aware of the salaries, business goals and marketing efforts of their colleagues?

With managed care, increased competition, and consumers who are more sophisticated with regard to mental health services, it is imperative that private practitioners avoid taking a passive approach to developing, promoting and maintaining their practices. There is little reason for competent, ethical and professional psychotherapists not to have profitable practices. Yet, achieving and maintaining this will require that, in addition to having good clinical skill, he or she will devote time, money and energy toward marketing their services.

Marketing

Marketing is a term used to describe proactive efforts an individual takes to promote his or her business and services. Marketing means more than buying a Yellow Page listing or placing an ad in the local newspaper (Kostreski, 1997). Rather, marketing for health care providers means helping to protect the integrity of services in the changing health care delivery system while capitalizing on opportunities created by market changes (Burnette, 1997). Given how competitive the field of mental health is becoming, marketing is a strategy private practice therapists can use to distinguish their services from other providers.

Ours is a market-driven economy. Those who prosper in the market, including psychotherapists, start with the market and develop services responsive to market demand. For example, if a gay or lesbian psychotherapist wishes to have a private practice made up exclusively of sexual minorities, he or she will need to ascertain the need for these services in his or her area. If this psychotherapist establishes a practice in a large, urban area, there should be little difficulty having the practice he or she desires. If, on the other hand, this psychotherapist works in a small, rural community, there may not be enough gay and lesbian persons wanting psychological services. Taken from this perspective, having a successful private practice requires psychotherapists to start with the market–the consumers who are likely to use his or her services and work backward.

A general rule of thumb is that the more service-oriented a business is, the more marketing will depend upon word-of-mouth advertising and professional referral rather than on media advertising to be effective (Beigel & Earle, 1990). Since much of what psychotherapists offer are services, not goods, the ability to cater one's practice to the community will determine which private practices make it and which do not.

The Marketing Plan

Many psychotherapists haphazardly embark on establishing a private practice. Perhaps they already have a few clients, have money saved for office space, and have generated some ideas about what kinds of ads they want to run. What is often missing, however, is a step-by-step plan of action for how their business will develop and grow. Many mistakenly believe that their reputations alone will take care of them. But while a good reputation provides the foundation for a successful practice, it is only a foundation, not an active marketing plan for gaining new clients (Shenson, 1994).

The overall goal in business planning is to think everything through; to have answers to problems before they develop. Business planning requires that the private practitioner be willing to prepare for everything–even failure.

Approximately 50 percent of professional practices fail within the first three years. Shenson (1994) suggests that this is often due to the following reasons:

- Inability of some professionals to function successfully on their own.
- Unwillingness or inability to market their services.
- Failure to market with consistency and regularity.
- High overhead or fiscal imprudence.
- Failure to expand at an appropriate rate and at the right time.

Marketing is a three-tiered process of analysis, goal setting, and implementation. As Beigel and Earle (1990) write, "Your personality determines the style of your marketing strategies while your marketable qualities and the service of therapy supply the content of the marketing plan" (p. 67).

Analysis

Before promoting a private practice, three features must be attended to. First, one must take stock of his or her credentials and experience. Second, time must be spent thinking about what kinds of clients the therapist wants to see. Third, one must determine how many therapists are working with the same type of clients.

By examining one's credentials and experiences, therapists are in a better position of being able to determine what types of clients are desired. For example, gay and lesbian therapists often have a desire to work with sexual minorities, but this need not happen at the expense of seeing other types of clients. If someone has experience in the fields of child therapy, chemical dependency, or trauma, there is no reason why a practice cannot reflect this diversity. Asking oneself what kinds of clients he or she does or does not want to see is therefore crucial to the overall plan.

Once the kind of clients one wishes to have in their psychotherapy practice is identified, the next challenge is figuring out how many of these people are in the town or city in which the clinician will be practicing. Libraries often have books containing census figures on a town's population. This includes average income, the number of single persons, average age, etc. Unfortunately, these resources do not identify the percentage of the community who are gay or lesbian. Clinicians will therefore need to find creative ways of obtaining this information.

One way to approximate the number of gays and lesbians in a particular community is to ask the editor of a local gay or lesbian publication, or manager of a gay or lesbian bar, how many people either read the paper or patronize the club. This information, along with the fact that the community even has these resources, can give clinicians important data. Also, it stands to follow that towns having a variety of gay and lesbian services will have a higher percentage of sexual minorities.

Identifying other therapists who work with similar types of clients is necessary. In theory, if there are four psychotherapists in a community who see a certain kind of client (e.g., gay or lesbian), with proper marketing each person's profitability should be at least one quarter.

Rather than viewing other therapists as competition, it is more helpful to see one another as potential sources of support and referral. By exchanging information about backgrounds, experience, and types of service provided with other therapists, the chances of having a satisfying private practice are increased.

Goal Setting

Goals refer to the objectives one has for their practice. This includes determining how many clients are desired, maximum caseload, average monthly salary, and the date for the achievement of these goals. For example, if a therapist currently has four clients, but wants to have ten, he or she must decide how to make potential clients aware of his or her services. They should also decide by what date they want to have these six more clients. By knowing what their goals and timelines are, therapists can then work on strategies to achieve these goals.

In order for marketing objectives to be effective and useful, they must include measurable outcomes. Dates, number of clients, and financial expectations must all be clearly spelled out. This way, if a practitioner does not meet his or her goals, he or she can look back and see why this did not happen. On the other hand, quietly wondering why new referrals have not come in does not offer any useful information.

Implementation

Once a clinician has decided upon what kind of practice to have, specified the desired number of clients, established timelines and developed an understanding of the competition, he or she is ready to offer their psychological services to the community. Clinicians may want to simultaneously contact service organizations that cater to new businesses. Local branches of the Small Business Administration, for example, can help with securing loans and offer general tips on running a business. Business groups such as the Chamber of Commerce are helpful at keeping practitioners abreast of trends in the local business community.

Some private practices develop quite rapidly, while others are slow to grow. By continuously using a variety of marketing techniques, clinicians can maximize the potential of their own private practices.

MARKETING STRATEGIES

There is no formula for marketing a private practice. The only important variable is that the clinician makes marketing a priority, and that a percentage of time each week is devoted to analyzing and implementing one's marketing plan. Many therapists are familiar with the term *networking* and many believe that knowing other therapists or joining professional membership groups is enough. But in the changing climate of health care delivery, creativity in marketing is key.

What follows are examples of marketing techniques that can be used to develop and promote almost any kind of private practice.

The Open House

One option for informing colleagues about the work a clinician does is to host an open house. This can be done when the practice first opens, when the practice is moved to a different location, or when a new group member joins a practice. The open house is primarily designed to offer refreshments and opportunities for socializing or networking to other professionals in the community. It also permits the therapist to inform others about his or her practice. It can be helpful to invite diverse groups of professionals such as doctors, lawyers and staff from local mental health and medical clinics to the open house, as they can be valuable sources of referral.

Community Involvement

Joining business groups in the community is an effective way for therapists to make others aware of their psychological services. A glance at the roster of groups such as the Chamber of Commerce shows that few therapists actually utilize the opportunity for joining these groups. This fact alone maximizes the opportunity for therapists to bring more attention to their work. Typically, professional organizations such as the Chamber of Commerce require only that you be a businessperson in the local community.

Business groups often publish newsletters which highlight the work and activities of the membership, and many permit members to speak or distribute brochures at monthly meetings. This is an opportunity for therapists to talk about their work, trends in mental health counseling, or topics that might apply to a wide range of group members.

Several communities are also seeing the growth of gay and lesbian business associations. Basically a gay and lesbian chamber of commerce, these groups can provide therapists great opportunity for informing members of the community about their services.

Many newspapers also carry columns that include information on businesses in the community. Therapists can send in announcements pertaining to their practices to be included with other listings. This is a particularly useful forum for receiving free publicity about workshops, support groups, open houses, new group members, specialty services, etc.

Writing

Few things get clinicians noticed more rapidly in their community than the ability to write or publish. People understand information they are able to see. Writing on the field of mental health need not be a permanent commitment, however. Many local newspapers will accept articles by mental health professionals who can write on timely material. A good time to submit written material to the local press is when social or political events bring gay and lesbian issues to the general media, for example, when a famous person comes out, when equal rights for gays and lesbians are being discussed, etc.

The gay and lesbian press is often void of mental health articles, and therapists have much to offer in this area. Even though many newspapers are not able to offer adequate financial compensation for articles, writing is a good way of establishing and maintaining name recognition for one's private practice.

Public Speaking

Depending upon the clinical expertise of the therapist, several schools and groups might have an interest in hearing a brief presentation. With increased focus on gay and lesbian youth, for example, therapists familiar with these issues can offer to speak at parent or teachers' groups. Colleges that offer courses on health, sexuality or general psychology might also find it useful to hear a therapist talk on topics pertaining to mental health.

As services for gays and lesbians diversify, therapists can also take advantage of speaking to gay and lesbian professionals' groups, on gay and lesbian radio programs, and to churches and social groups.

Contacting Large Businesses

In 1996, the Practice Directorate of the American Psychological Association surveyed 490 U.S. employers, asking about their use of and satisfaction with behavioral health services (Burnette & Sleek, 1997). Most of the 82 respondents, representing 2.27 million employees, said they want data on how the provision of psychological services affects employee productivity and absenteeism. This presents a great opportunity for therapists to contact businesses in the community, offering to do training or education for staff on mental health issues.

With more businesses trying to exercise sensitivity to ethnic, gender and cultural differences in their employees, gay and lesbian therapists can be vital resources. Offering to do diversity training in the workplace is a terrific opportunity for private practitioners, since training can be scheduled during times when the therapist is not otherwise seeing patients.

Finally, as Powers (1996) points out, many businesses fail to attain optimum performance from the approximately ten percent of their population who are sexual minorities. This, Powers maintains, is because expending energy on non-work related items, such as finding ways to network, protecting themselves from abuse and discrimination, and feeling isolated detracts from effective job performance. When employers realize it is to their advantage to support gay and lesbian employees, their profits will rise. Private practitioners are therefore encouraged to approach the business community with offers to provide education, guidance and counseling in these areas.

Follow-Up with Referrals

Psychotherapy referrals come from a variety of sources. Clients will call a therapist, indicating they received the referral from another therapist, a physician, or a friend. It is extremely important that therapists keep track of who is referring to their practices. Establishing contact with referral sources, and offering feedback or appreciation, goes a long way toward securing future referrals.

People who refer a client to a therapist are interested in the results of their actions. Though laws pertaining to confidentiality prevent a therapist from offering details to the referring party about the client, it is appropriate to let the other person know you were contacted by the person they referred. Alternately, therapists should notify other professionals when they make referrals to them.

Since many therapists list their services with local hospitals, clinics, and hot-lines, it is important to phone these places periodically to make sure the information they have about the practice is current and correct. This also keeps the therapist in contact with the staff and volunteers at these places who make referrals.

Creating Products

Though most therapists would not want to sell products from their office, there are other ways of providing tangible services to consumers. Currently there are over 150 bookstores in the U.S. that primarily sell books on topics of interest to gays and lesbians, as well as cards, magazines, and games. Private practitioners might want to consider ways of promoting their practices through these stores. For example, making audiotapes offering advice on a variety of issues of concern to gays and lesbians might encourage listeners to contact the therapist. Making sure brochures that include information about one's psychological services are placed in local alternative bookstores can also be useful.

Creating a Home Page

With more and more people using their computers as a resource in both their work and private life, therapists can find ways of promoting their practices on the World Wide Web. Creating a "home page" is one way of doing this. Information about support groups, therapy services, or general interest articles can all be included. Since many consumers are somewhat mystified by psychotherapy, including reader-friendly articles about therapy and the services provided in the community can help generate new referrals.

Keeping Track of Current Trends

Current events, particularly those that affect the people who live in the community where a private practitioner works, offer unique opportunities for clinicians. For example, when two gay men were attacked in a grocery store parking lot in a medium-sized city in Texas, a therapist in private practice made his services available to these men at no charge. He also spoke with local church leaders about how they could take steps to decrease hate crimes in their community. Though none of this was motivated by him trying to increase the number of psychotherapy referrals to his practice, efforts of this nature do have a positive impact on the life and work of psychotherapists.

Don't Go at It Alone

Private practice can be a rewarding experience, but at times it can feel quite isolating. Nowadays, it is not possible to separate one's practice from the larger health care community. Rather, because of increased needs for marketing, cross-referral, networking, and professional growth and satisfaction, practitioners need to stay active in their field and community. Even though private practice may be the job of choice for some, it is necessary to recognize that private practitioners are part of the greater whole.

It is important that therapists know the work of their colleagues, and that they share information about their own practices with other health professionals. Inevitably, therapists get asked for referrals to other therapists by friends, co-workers, and neighbors. By being familiar with the services offered by other therapists, their fee arrangements, and the kinds of clients with whom they work, therapists can confidently give referrals when asked. Taking the time to get this information from other therapists also encourages them to do the same.

Think Like a Businessperson

Therapists should consider taking courses offered through community colleges or business associations on running a business. It is important for therapists to recognize that there are trends in private practice, just as there are trends in retail stores. This includes seasonal highs and lows, periods of time when referrals are not as frequent, and the realization that client needs don't always coincide with therapist financial considerations.

By becoming aware of financial planning, investment options, working with insurance companies, and flexible fee schedules, therapists maximize their opportunity for making private practice a financially rewarding endeavor.

CONCLUSION

Managed care and increased competition do not mean that clinicians cannot have successful private practices. Yet, in order to sustain a private practice, mental health professionals must learn to incorporate the role of entrepreneur into their identities. Treating a private practice as a business does not mean that clients are given sub-standard care. Rather, it shows that the practitioner is committed to his or her work, and is willing to do what is necessary to make independent practice work in today's health care marketplace.

REFERENCES

Adams, J. (1987). A brave new world for private practice? *The Family Therapy Networker.* January/February, 18-25.

Beigel, J.K., & Earle, R.H. (1990). *Successful private practice in the 1990s.* New York: Brunner/Mazel, Inc.

Bradford, J., & Ryan, C. (1987). *National lesbian health care survey: Mental health implications.* Richmond, VA: Virginia Commonwealth University Research Laboratory.

Bradford, J., Ryan, C., & Rothblum, E.D. (1994). National lesbian health care survey: Implications for mental health care. *Journal of Consulting and Clinical Psychology,* 62 (2), 228-242.

Burnette, E. (1997). Novel marketing strategies boost psychologist referrals. *American Psychological Association Monitor,* March, 36.

Burnette, E., & Sleek, S. (1997). Network aids psychologists with their business needs. *American Psychological Association Monitor,* March, 36.

Cardea, C. (1985). The lesbian revolution and the 50-minute hour: A working-class look at therapy and the movement. *Lesbian Ethics,* 1(3), 46-68.

Hoagland, S.L. (1988). *Lesbian ethics: Toward new value.* Palo Alto, CA: Institute of Lesbian Studies.

Kostreski, F. (1997). Fee-for-service success relies on good marketing. *Family Practice News,* April, 1997, 84.

Modrcin, M.J., & Wyers, N.L. (1990). Lesbian and gay couples: Where they turn when help is needed. *Journal of Gay & Lesbian Psychotherapy,* 1(3), 89-104.

Morgan, K.S. (1992). Caucasian lesbians' use of psychotherapy. *Psychology of Women Quarterly,* 16, 127-130.

Powers, B. (1996). *Sexual identity on the job.* New York: The Haworth Press, Inc.

Rudolph, J. (1988). Counselors' attitudes toward homosexuality: A selective review of the literature. *Journal of Counseling and Development,* 67, 165-168.

Shenson, H.L. (1994). *Shenson on consulting: Success from the consultant's consultant.* New York: John Wiley and Sons.

Lesbian Therapists and Lesbian Clients: Therapeutic and Practical Considerations, with Implications for Private Practice

Pamm Hanson
Pamela Weeks

SUMMARY. The authors, on the basis of their own experience, explore issues specific to therapists working openly as lesbians with lesbian clients. Their discussion covers the structure of a private practice, the therapeutic relationship between lesbian therapist and lesbian client, and personal challenges for the lesbian therapist. Questions are raised and direction given with the aim of facilitating congruence among the therapist's personal capacities, the therapeutic setting, and the psychological intention of the therapeutic work. The authors note the therapist's need to tolerate the exposure of her personal life and the pressure toward fusion that are both entailed in work with lesbian clients, and they suggest that these special challenges, when the lesbian therapist's

---

Pamm Hanson, MA, is a certified mental health professional currently providing psychotherapy and consultation in private practice. Pamela Weeks, MA, is also in private practice, seeing couples and individuals. Both work openly as lesbians in Seattle. Both have also served as administrators, Pamela Weeks as the first director of Seattle's Lesbian Resource Center and Pamm Hanson as executive director of Seattle Counseling Service for Sexual Minorities, the oldest gay and lesbian mental health center in the country.

Address correspondence to the authors in care of Pamm Hanson, Pioneer Building, Suite 523, 600 First Avenue, Seattle, WA 98104.

The authors thank Mary Holscher, PhD, for substantive contributions, Xavier Callahan for editorial comments on an earlier draft, and "all of us who muck about in complex lesbian relationships."

[Haworth co-indexing entry note]: "Lesbian Therapists and Lesbian Clients: Therapeutic and Practical Considerations, with Implications for Private Practice." Hanson, Pamm and Pamela Weeks. Co-published simultaneously in *Journal of Gay & Lesbian Social Services* (The Haworth Press, Inc.) Vol. 8, No. 4, 1998, pp. 43-57; and: *Working with Gay Men and Lesbians in Private Psychotherapy Practice* (ed: Christopher J. Alexander) The Haworth Press, Inc., 1998, pp. 43-57. Single or multiple copies of this article are available for a fee from The Haworth Document Delivery Service [1-800-342-9678, 9:00 a.m. - 5:00 p.m. (EST). E-mail address: getinfo@haworthpressinc.com].

43

engagement with them is conscious, offer rich material that can deepen the therapeutic relationship and the therapeutic work. *[Article copies available for a fee from The Haworth Document Delivery Service: 1-800-342-9678. E-mail address: getinfo@haworthpressinc.com]*

Our experience as openly lesbian therapists working with lesbian clients since the early 1970s has given us certain insights into some special issues and challenges that arise in the practice of psychotherapy with this client population, particularly when the therapist is in private practice. One theme running consistently through these issues and challenges is the need for congruence between the lesbian therapist's intentions and the actual dynamics of her work with lesbian clients. What this means in practice is congruence among several factors, including but not limited to the following capacities and choices on the part of the therapist:

- Her personal capacity for tolerating the distortions of transference and undertaking critical self-reflection
- Her political capacity, as expressed in part through her ability and willingness to engage with and assimilate negative as well as positive aspects of being a social outsider
- Her choice of geographical location and physical setting for her therapy office
- Her choices about the psychological direction of her therapeutic work with clients

This article offers an overview of issues that any openly lesbian therapist may want to consider in finding and maintaining that kind of congruence. Nevertheless, we hope that the information presented here will be especially helpful to lesbian therapists in private practice, and that it will suggest opportunities for anticipating conflicts and difficulties, making informed choices, and deepening the therapeutic work with lesbian clients. The article concludes with suggestions for further research.

ISSUES IN ESTABLISHING A PRIVATE PRACTICE WITH LESBIAN CLIENTS

As Berman (1985) notes, problems may arise whenever any therapist serves any kind of subcommunity or works in a small-town context; and, in our experience, being an "out" lesbian therapist working with lesbian clients in the lesbian community is like being a therapist in a small town. As long as the therapist is known to the lesbian community as a lesbian–even if her client population is not exclusively lesbian, and even if she has her practice in a large city–the portion of her personal life that is carried on in public is susceptible to the same kind of exposure that characterizes the personal life of a small-town therapist.

Privacy and Confidentiality

The exposure to which the openly lesbian therapist is subject may extend to her private personal history, especially if she has come of age or lived for any length of time in the city or area where she has her practice. Very often in the lesbian community there is shared knowledge, even a kind of myth, about the therapist's "wild youth," or perhaps about her life in the suburbs before coming out as a lesbian or having her lesbian identity otherwise come to light (for example, perhaps it was revealed in the course of her political activities).

The "out" lesbian therapist is also more publicly visible to her lesbian clients than most other therapists are to their clients (Anthony, 1982; Cerbone, 1991; Falco, 1991). A politically active lesbian therapist, for instance, may be motivated by deeply held personal values, and her activism may allow her to provide a positive role model for her clients (Anthony, 1982; Rochlin, 1985), but she may find that the personal is political indeed as her private values become a focus of clients' curiosity and discussion. Moreover, lesbian cultural events that attract the participation of both the therapist and her clients are also settings where the therapist's friends and lovers are on display, and where her substance use or abstinence can be observed.

The issue of client and therapist seeing each other in public has to be addressed at the outset with all lesbian clients. The initial session is a good time for the therapist to present her protocol and develop agreed-upon expectations with the client. Their discussion should address questions like these:

- If the client and the therapist see each other in public, who initiates contact?
- What are the expectations for how personal introductions will be handled?

- Is the encounter to be seen as a topic for discussion in therapy or not?

Each therapist must answer these questions for herself and clarify them with her lesbian clients.

The openly lesbian therapist's greater visibility to her lesbian clients does have specifically therapeutic implications, of course. As one example, especially in view of the lesbian community's need for positive images and role models (Nichols, 1987), clients may idealize the therapist and thus be unable to tolerate what could be viewed as her lapses from ideal conduct (Anthony, 1982). As another example, personal contact between therapist and client outside the therapy setting can complicate the analysis of transference (Anthony, 1982), and so the therapist may have to tolerate the feeling of being distorted and intruded upon until the therapeutic alliance is personal enough and strong enough for her to use the transference as rich material for therapy. We will examine other such implications shortly (see "Roles and Boundaries," below.)

In any event, the proverbial six degrees of separation become three or even two in the lesbian community. As happens whenever any group is stigmatized as a minority, individuals of diverse personality types, interests, and lifestyles are thrown together by a common label and common concerns. In the lesbian community, however, social circles and friendship networks frequently cross boundaries of race and class as well. Therefore, the lesbian therapist who is meeting a prospective lesbian client in the initial interview can assume (even if she may not be able to anticipate) at least some degree of overlap between the prospective client's social or friendship networks and the social or friendship networks of other clients. One consequence of this overlap is that even when two clients belong to societal or demographic groups so disparate that any overlap between them would be remarkable in a context other than the lesbian community, the therapist may hear, and be required to hold, information from one client that is pertinent but unknown to the other (Falco, 1991). A second consequence is that the therapist may hear of another client's involvement in a twelve-step program, with the concomitant loss of that client's anonymity. And, as the therapist often comes to realize, these and other consequences may well reach into her own private life, if her clients or people in her clients' lives are acquainted with people in her own social and friendship networks.

The openly lesbian therapist, by definition, has already rejected the closet as a solution to this invasion of her privacy. Another potential solution is isolation–a not infrequent outcome for lesbian therapists who are grappling with questions of privacy and invasion. But isolation is not an authentic solution. The lesbian therapist has to realize that her private life can and will enter therapy–directly or indirectly, and probably sooner rather than later. She must come to terms with this level of exposure and decide how best to accept it while making the conscious choice to respect her own personal need for affiliation in the larger lesbian community.

The Private Practice's Structure, Setting, and Economic Viability

The issues discussed so far are not unique to lesbian therapists in private practice; openly lesbian therapists working with lesbian clients in agencies or other clinical settings also face this sort of exposure and must cope with the same pressures on confidentiality. But the openly lesbian therapist in private practice confronts an additional dilemma: How will she come to terms with invasion of her privacy, maintain her therapeutic commitment to her clients' privacy and confidentiality, and operate her practice as a viable business despite interference from the lesbian community's fluid social boundaries (Brown, 1984)?

The solution to this dilemma will encompass several questions that, although they are concrete and practical, are also complex and interdependent. The therapist's decision about where to have her office is partly predicated on her goals for her client load, goals that in turn will determine her choice of referral sources, a choice that hinges partly on the therapist's honest evaluation of how much public exposure she can tolerate. Because her decisions in these areas will become issues in her work with lesbian clients, the therapist must approach these questions with an unusual degree of scrupulous self-knowledge.

Where exposure of personal information is concerned, the therapist can adopt a proactive stance. Disclosure statements, introductory brochures, and advertising materials can serve as vehicles for communicating personal information that is relevant to her work with lesbian clients, or even for defusing information that could distract from the goals of therapy if discovered accidentally (information, for example, about the therapist's political activism, her involvement in arts or service organizations, her participation in such community institutions as choirs, sports teams, and so forth).

When the question is one of client population and referral sources, the therapist can seek to minimize social overlap between her clients by conducting outreach to a variety of different groups in the lesbian community. She can also restrict lesbian clients to a certain percentage of her total client population and encourage referrals from other populations. Another possibility is to conduct outreach on a topic of expertise and interest that focuses on a specific therapeutic issue or technique (EMDR, writer's block, chemical dependency) rather than on a particular population of clients. With any and all of these approaches, however, the therapist must still assume that some social overlap will occur because it is inevitable in the lesbian community.

The therapist's choice about where to have her office must be congruent with what she has identified for herself as a comfortable degree of "outness," as well as with her decision about whether to direct her practice primarily toward lesbian clients. Most cities have gay- or liberal-identified neighborhoods; most cities also have more neutral commercial areas that carry no associations regarding particular social groups or political beliefs. On the one hand, having a therapy office in a gay-identified or gay-friendly neighborhood can promote lesbian clients' sense of belonging to a larger community and help decrease their feelings of societal rejection (Perlman, 1987). On the other hand, having the office in a strongly lesbian-identified neighborhood may intimidate women who are confused or unsure about questions of lifestyle or sexual orientation, and so the therapist's practice may be limited by default to women who are completely comfortable with an "out" lesbian identification.

As for the office itself, it is important to recognize that its furnishings, artwork, reading material, and so on, will convey messages about the therapist's values and politics and may foster expectations and assumptions about the client's and the therapist's shared experience. The relationship between an openly lesbian therapist and a lesbian client is one that is freighted from the start with issues of fusion (see "Fusion, Transference, and the Therapeutic Alliance," below). For this reason, choices about the waiting room's decor and amenities offer an opportunity for the therapist to balance two goals: the goal of helping the client feel comfortable and accepted, and the goal of basing the therapeutic relationship more on the developing therapeutic alliance than on implicit assumptions of similarity between therapist and client. Balancing these two goals is a task that evokes very personal questions for each therapist.

SPECIAL ISSUES IN THE THERAPEUTIC RELATIONSHIP

The concerns discussed in this section are predominantly theoretical, and they may not seem personal enough for therapy. The lesbian therapist does need to make room for them, however, because an exclusive focus on the client's personal and psychological issues can limit the scope and strength of therapeutic change, especially when both therapist and client are members of an oppressed minority (Cerbone, 1991). As we will see, factors that derive from expectations of interpersonal equality, from the relative fluidity of roles and boundaries in the lesbian community, from clients' assumptions of shared experience with the therapist, and from the high incidence of fusion in intimate lesbian relationships can bring considerable pressure to bear on the therapeutic relationship between a lesbian client and an openly lesbian therapist.

The Balance of Power

Living as a lesbian means facing personal and political questions about one's place in society, questions that revolve around acceptance and exclusion. These questions extend into the lesbian community as well, where issues of class, ethnicity, race, disability, and other factors come into play, just as they do in the larger society.

Of necessity, then, lesbians' sensitivity to interpersonal power dynamics and imbalances is often quite acute, and lesbian clients not infrequently develop considerable sophistication with interpersonal language and process. As a result, they may come to therapy with expectations of interpersonal equality (Burch, 1987; McCandlish, 1982; Peplau, Pedesky, & Hamilton, 1982; Schneider, 1986). These expectations often have to be revised, however, given the therapist's assumptions about her own authority in the therapeutic situation, as well as her very real alliance with sources of institutional power (see "Dealing with Community-Based Pressures," below).

Roles and Boundaries

Lesbian clients, even if they are emotionally shut down or psychologically naïve, are often highly skilled at creating relationships rather than adhering blindly to prescribed roles. Lesbians as a community are not under the sway of the conventions that tend to be taken for granted among heterosexuals (Clunis and Green, 1988). For example, lesbians' most intimate friendships are very often with their past lovers (Elise, 1991), and most lesbians have had personal experience of dual relationships entailing intimate involvement. As a result, the lesbian community is accustomed to encompassing many kinds of complex relationships in social and political groups (Falco, 1991).

The lesbian client, then, is already comparatively unrestricted by conventional roles when she enters therapy. Because she is often used to questioning or challenging prescribed roles, her lesbian therapist cannot look to the socially accepted mores of the therapeutic relationship for protection from what may prove to be an uncomfortable encounter. The encounter can be uncomfortable for the client, too, as Elise (1991, pp. 63-64) notes in her discussion of special issues for lesbians eroticizing intimate relationships:

> Due to anxiety over erotic feelings toward girlfriends all through [the] teen years . . . lesbians often [have] not had the experience of highly intimate, but clearly platonic, "girlfriend" relationships. Instead, all girlfriends become lovers and eventually most love relationships then develop into friendships. Thus, the therapy relationship is often the first situation where intimacy occurs without sexuality–an uncomfortable experience for women who have been familiar with intimacy mainly in the context of feeling sexually powerful.

The lesbian client's relative lack of restriction to conventional roles can clearly be a strength (Pardie & Herb, 1997), but it may also put pressure on the therapist with respect to the boundaries of the therapeutic relationship. This sort of pressure can announce itself in more than one way. We have already discussed some boundary-related ramifications of the lesbian community's intricate social and friendship networks. Another manifestation of the pressure on therapeutic boundaries can be seen in the lesbian client who has contradictory needs for containment and rebellion and who expresses these needs by challenging and pushing against the therapist. Some boundaries delineate the needs and welfare of the client; others delineate the needs and welfare of the therapist. But choices about boundaries must always "imply and demand acknowledgement of the primacy of the client's needs in the therapy relationship" (Cerbone, 1991, p. 50). The therapist, to the extent that she can tolerate pressure on the boundaries of the therapeutic relationship, can use this pressure in uncovering therapeutic issues and in learning how to see the client's reactions and her own as material for expanding and deepening the therapy.

The issue of roles and boundaries may arise especially at termination (Kupers, 1988). The ultimate goal of therapy is separation, but, as we have seen (Elise, 1986, 1991), the lesbian client may have personal experience of transforming separation into a new kind of continuing relationship, as when a lover becomes a best friend. There are profound and spiritual issues at stake in termination, and they can be explored if the therapist and the client are able to go deeply into questions of separation and connection, fusion, and individuation.

Fusion, Transference, and the Therapeutic Alliance

We alluded earlier to the lesbian client's possible expectations and assumptions about what she and her openly lesbian therapist have in common (see "The Private Practice's Structure, Setting, and Economic Viability," above), as well as to what is often a salient characteristic of lesbian relationships: fusion (Krestan & Bepko, 1980), or merger (McKenzie, 1992). A telling phrase, whether it comes from the client or the therapist, is "She really knows me!"

Assumptions of commonality between lesbian client and lesbian therapist–expectations about values, politics, and personal experience, for example–can accelerate the building of trust and the therapeutic alliance (Perlman, 1987). They can also accelerate transference, and possibly countertransference as well (de Montflores, 1986; Elise, 1991; Seligson, 1977). The enhanced trust is positive, but the accelerated transference may feel intrusive to the therapist. As such, it may lead her to set boundaries earlier in the therapeutic relationship than she would with a nonlesbian client (Anthony, 1982; Cohen & Stein, 1986). These early boundaries may lead to conflict if the client feels bewildered or startled by them, or if she perceives them as a betrayal of shared experience. And if, as Perlman (1987) suggests, the client's assumptions of commonality have accelerated the transference, then the ensuing conflict will occur at a time when the therapeutic alliance may be weaker and more tentative than would ideally be the case.

It must be remembered, however, that the client may not be the only one bringing assumptions of shared experience to the therapeutic encounter. To take just one example, lesbian therapists who seek training, consultation, or professional development can easily identify their own experience with that of a prospective lesbian client in search of a therapist: lesbian clients may work at times with therapists familiar with the psychological aspects of problems but unfamiliar with lesbian life, just as lesbian therapists must learn to take information from topic-specific training and translate it into their own particular context. Lesbian clients and lesbian therapists both need someone–a therapist in one case, a trainer or consultant in the other–who can respond to their needs with due consideration of lesbian-specific issues, but without undue distraction by irrelevant ideas and feelings about lesbianism.

But the lesbian therapist's challenges are not all centered on matters of theory and technique. Despite the danger of assumptions and fusion, it must also be remembered that the lesbian therapist does indeed share a deep experience with the lesbian client: the experience of being on the outside of the greater society, and on the inside of a subcommunity. This shared experience may work for or against the lesbian therapist, but it will always challenge her in her personal and psychological development.

PERSONAL CHALLENGES FOR THE LESBIAN THERAPIST

Throughout his work, Searles (1989) stresses the importance of the therapist's developing a countertransference that corresponds with and informs the client's transference. To put this idea another way, the client can go only as deeply into therapy as the therapist can tolerate. Therefore, the lesbian therapist needs to acknowledge the reality of her personal limitations so that she can form mutual, respectful relationships with her clients (Maroda, 1991). She must also develop an awareness of her own personal capacity for negotiating the sometimes opposed expectations of the lesbian and therapeutic communities.

Working with Internalized Homophobia and Personal Defenses

Minority status imposes and enforces the painful experience of being marginalized. In response to this experience, lesbians may develop strong defenses whose function is to protect them from the hurt of oppression and exclusion, defenses that may also function to express the homophobia internalized from the larger society's attitudes and behavior. Certain forms of internalized homophobia, such as alcoholism, may be easier to spot than others, such as excessive devotion to work or athletics (see Margolies, Becker, & Jackson-Brewer, 1987, for some of the less obvious expressions of internalized homophobia and their underlying defenses). The less obvious expressions of internalized homophobia may be all the more difficult for a lesbian therapist to identify if she herself engages in them—all the more reason for her to arrange for regular consultation and case review, thereby providing for herself the kind of challenges and scrutiny that are built into therapeutic work conducted in agencies and group practices.

But if minority status is painful, it also offers the outsider access to a rich history of the minority group's resistance to oppression, a unique tapestry of the group's culture, and the inspiration available from engaging with both. For therapist and client alike, however, using these resources may mean unearthing and grappling with internalized homophobia (Margolies, Becker, & Jackson-Brewer, 1987), and unless the lesbian therapist makes a conscious effort to do so, she may be colluding with her clients to solidify unconscious defenses against external and internalized homophobia. As a result, both she and her clients may miss the opportunity to grow stronger and more creative in confronting and living with injustice.

The therapist also has to make every effort to rid herself of unrealistic expectations and must work continuously toward an awareness of those personal defenses that may create blind spots and defensiveness in her work with clients. For example, a lesbian client may need the space to examine and express any loss and grief she may feel over being a woman who does not fit the stereotype for women in our society (Baron, 1996; Elliott, 1985); indeed, recognition of this loss, and of her consequent grieving, may be crucial to her deep acceptance of herself as a lesbian (Thompson, 1996). Therefore, the therapeutic repertoire of the lesbian therapist cannot be limited to celebrations of the joy and freedom of lesbian self-acceptance; the therapist herself needs the ability to recognize, accept, and tolerate hearing about the "shadow" aspects of being an outsider.

Dealing with Community-Based Pressures

Both the lesbian community and the therapeutic community can exert great demands and pressures in terms of ethics and mores. The lesbian therapist may feel accountable to each of the associated sets of expectations, and any deviation from either set may incur harsh social or professional judgments or even penalties.

Sometimes the expectations of the two communities overlap, and concerns are intensified around certain issues. For example, because both the lesbian community and the therapeutic community are sensitive to inappropriate sexual behavior within the therapeutic relationship, it becomes a highly charged topic for the lesbian therapist. There are also times when the expectations of the two communities are in conflict. For example, the lesbian community tends toward suspicion of authority, mistrust of established power structures, and contradictory feelings about dependency (Burch, 1987), whereas the therapeutic community has spoken and unspoken assumptions about the therapist's authority, as well as an alliance with existing power structures. Regardless of the strength or nature of the pressure from either the lesbian or the therapeutic community, sexual issues in the therapeutic work need to be addressed from a thoughtful therapeutic stance, not just from a reactive stance toward the community pressure attending the lesbian therapist's two primary identifications (as a lesbian and as a therapist). And even though a lesbian therapist may be experiencing conflict over her own alliance with existing power structures, this conflict may also prompt her to pursue a healthy critical examination of her own personal authority. (See Falco, 1991, for the skills and abilities that will serve a therapist in applying her experiences as a lesbian to therapeutic issues and to her work in therapy.)

CONCLUSION AND DIRECTIONS FOR FURTHER RESEARCH

Our experience over the past two decades has convinced us of the need for congruence between the openly lesbian therapist's intentions and the actual dynamics that are present in her work with lesbian clients. In view of that need, and in view of the need for the deeper understanding that supports this kind of congruence, we have tried in this article to offer insights into the therapeutic relationship that an openly lesbian therapist can and should establish with a lesbian client. In so doing, we have discussed factors ranging from the therapist's personal and political capacities to the location of the therapy office and the direction of the therapeutic work. Our discussion has encompassed special issues that affect openly lesbian therapists working with lesbian clients in private practice, general issues involved in any therapeutic relationship between an openly lesbian therapist and a lesbian client, and personal challenges for the lesbian therapist who works with lesbian clients.

Although we hope that the information presented here will be helpful to other openly lesbian therapists, particularly those in private practice, we recognize that a number of issues still need further and continuing exploration and discussion. Here are some topics that we hope others will be inspired to take up:

- Relationships between lesbian therapists (as friends, lovers, colleagues, and so forth), and the implications of those relationships for work in therapy
- Special and unique issues pertaining to relationships between lesbian therapists and lesbian clients that cross the conventional emotional and sexual boundaries of therapy, especially in connection with termination
- Factors affecting decisions about how "out" to be in the psychotherapeutic community and in the work with clients
- Special issues in the therapeutic relationship between a lesbian therapist and a heterosexual woman client
- Issues and special burdens that lesbian therapists face in seeking consultation or topic-specific training and professional development, including exploration and discussion of the following related questions:
  - The trade-off between, on the one hand, lesbian therapists' joining formally or informally with other lesbian therapists to support the process of "translating" information into a lesbian context, and, on the other hand, the risk that the lesbian therapists will become isolated from the larger training group
  - The question of whether and how the inclusion of sexual-orientation issues in training can offer insight into therapeutic work with all kinds of clients, raising questions that illumi-

nate universal features of psychological development and interpersonal dynamics
- The question of how lesbian therapists can balance, on the one hand, the risk and effort of educating others about the lesbian context and, on the other, the safety and comfort of personal retreat and self-protection
- The issue of whether and how the movement toward diversity training in business and education can provide information about balancing the comforts of sameness and the challenges of difference, and whether this information can prove relevant to therapeutic and social service systems.

REFERENCES

Anthony, B. (1982). Lesbian client-lesbian therapist: Opportunities and challenges in working together. *Journal of Homosexuality, 7*(2/3), 45-49.

Baron, J. (1996). Some issues in psychotherapy with gay and lesbian clients. *Psychotherapy, 33*(4), 611-616.

Berman, J.R.S. (1985). Ethical feminist perspectives in dual relationships with clients. In L.B. Rosewater & L.E.A. Walker (Eds.), *Handbook of feminist therapy* (pp. 287-296). New York: Springer.

Brown, L. (1984). The lesbian feminist therapist in private practice and her community. *Psychotherapy in Private Practice, 2*(4), 9-16.

Burch, B. (1987). Barriers to intimacy: Conflicts over power, dependency, and nurturing in lesbian relationships. In Boston Lesbian Psychologies Collective (Eds.), *Lesbian psychologies* (pp. 126-141). Urbana: University of Illinois Press.

Cerbone, A. (1991). The effects of political activism on psychotherapy: A case study. In C. Silverstein (Ed.), *Gays, lesbians, and their therapists* (pp. 40-51). New York: Norton.

Clunis, M., & Green, D. (1988). *Lesbian couples*. Seattle, WA: Seal Press.

Cohen, C.J., & Stein, T.S. (1986). Reconceptualizing individual psychotherapy with gay men and lesbians. In T.S. Stein & C.J. Cohen (Eds.), *Contemporary perspectives in psychotherapy with gay men and lesbians* (pp. 27-54). New York: Plenum.

de Montflores, C. (1986). Notes on the management of difference. In T.S. Stein & C.J. Cohen (Eds.), *Contemporary perspectives in psychotherapy with gay men and lesbians* (pp. 73-101). New York: Plenum.

Elise, D. (1986). Lesbian couples: The implications of sex differences in separation-individuation. *Psychotherapy, 23*(2), 305-310.

Elise, D. (1991). When sexual and romantic feelings permeate the therapeutic relationship. In C. Silverstein (Ed.), *Gays, lesbians, and their therapists* (pp. 52-67). New York: Norton.

Elliott, D.E. (1985). Theory and research on lesbian identity formation. *International Journal of Women's Studies, 8*(1), 64-71.

Falco, K. (1991). *Psychotherapy with lesbian clients*. New York: Brunner/Mazel.

Krestan, J., & Bepko, C.S. (1980). The problem of fusion in the lesbian relationship. *Family Process, 19*, 277-289.

Kupers, T. (1988). *Ending therapy.* New York: New York University Press.

McCandlish, B. (1982). Therapeutic issues with lesbian couples. In J.C. Gonsiorek (Ed.), *Homosexuality and psychotherapy: A practitioner's handbook of affirmative models* (pp. 71-78). Binghamton, NY: The Haworth Press, Inc.

McKenzie, S. (1992). Merger in lesbian relationships. *Women & Therapy, 12*(1/2), 151-160.

Margolies, L., Becker, M., & Jackson-Brewer, K. (1987). Internalized homophobia: Identifying and treating the oppressor within. In Boston Lesbian Psychologies Collective (Eds.), *Lesbian psychologies* (pp. 2290-241). Urbana: University of Illinois Press.

Maroda, K.J. (1991). *The power of counter-transference.* New York: Wiley.

Nichols, M. (1987). Doing sex therapy with lesbians: Bending a heterosexual paradigm to fit a gay life-style. In Boston Lesbian Psychologies Collective (Eds.), *Lesbian psychologies* (pp. 242-260). Urbana: University of Illinois Press.

Pardie, L., & Herb, C. (1997). Merger and fusion in lesbian relationships: A problem of diagnosing what's wrong in terms of what's right. *Women & Therapy, 20*(3), 51-61.

Peplau, L.A., Pedesky, C., & Hamilton, M. (1982). Satisfaction in lesbian relationships. *Journal of Homosexuality, 8*(2), 23-35.

Perlman, S. (1987). The saga of continuing clash in lesbian community, or will an army of ex-lovers fail? In Boston Lesbian Psychologies Collective (Eds.), *Lesbian psychologies* (pp. 313-326). Urbana: University of Illinois Press.

Rochlin, M. (1985). Sexual orientation of the therapist and therapeutic effectiveness with gay clients. In J.C. Gonsiorek (Ed.), *A guide to psychotherapy with gay and lesbian clients* (pp. 21-29). New York: Harrington Park Press.

Schneider, M.S. (1986). The relationships of cohabiting lesbian and heterosexual couples: A comparison. *Psychology of Women Quarterly, 10*, 234-239.

Searles, H. (1989, December). The psychodynamics of borderline patients. Paper presented at the Psychological Forum, "Psychoanalytic Psychotherapy with Borderline Patients," San Francisco.

Seligson, R. (1977). Internalization of the therapeutic alliance. *Psychotherapy: Theory, Research, and Practice, 14*, 242-244.

Thompson, C. (1996). Lesbian grief and loss issues in the coming-out process. In C. Alexander (Ed.), *Gay and lesbian mental health: A sourcebook for practitioners* (pp. 211-222). Binghamton, NY: The Haworth Press, Inc.

Clinical and Practical Considerations in Private Practice with Lesbians and Gay Men of Color

Richard A. Rodriguez

SUMMARY. The clinical and practical needs of people of color who come to private practitioners are diverse. Issues of coming out, spirituality, multiple identity, and gender role take on unique characteristics with persons of different racial and ethnic backgrounds. This chapter covers practical considerations clinicians are encouraged to stay mindful of when working with clients of different racial and cultural backgrounds, including social class, race, and boundary issues. *[Article copies available for a fee from The Haworth Document Delivery Service: 1-800-342-9678. E-mail address: getinfo@haworthpressinc.com]*

To fight homophobia and racism, we must continually challenge and push ourselves . . . Fighting homophobia need not involve physical struggle–often the greatest battles are psychological . . . The enemy within us is often more threatening than the enemies surrounding us . . . With all the efforts being made to divide minorities, it is important to remember that the real enemy is injustice, not each other.

–Keith Boykin (1996)

Richard A. Rodriguez, PhD, is a licensed psychologist in Northern California. In addition to a private clinical practice, he is a psychologist for student health services at UC Berkeley. He can be reached at UC Berkeley, Counseling and Psychological Services, 2222 Bancroft Way, Berkeley, CA 94720.

[Haworth co-indexing entry note]: "Clinical and Practical Considerations in Private Practice with Lesbians and Gay Men of Color." Rodriguez, Richard A. Co-published simultaneously in *Journal of Gay & Lesbian Social Services* (The Haworth Press, Inc.) Vol. 8, No. 4, 1998, pp. 59-75; and: *Working with Gay Men and Lesbians in Private Psychotherapy Practice* (ed: Christopher J. Alexander) The Haworth Press, Inc., 1998, pp. 59-75. Single or multiple copies of this article are available for a fee from The Haworth Document Delivery Service [1-800-342-9678, 9:00 a.m. - 5:00 p.m. (EST). E-mail address: getinfo@haworth pressinc.com].

INTRODUCTION

I have been a therapist for the last 10 years working in both agency and private practice settings and have noticed that in any era of psychology, particular themes stand out. Given the zeitgeist of the times, the terms "diversity," "cross-cultural counseling" and "multi-cultural counseling" have become common buzzwords in the mental health field, with little agreement on definition of terms, theoretical perspectives, and worldview. Often diversity is defined by the social, political, and economic forces in the setting in which we practice. Ultimately these forces influence who we see, how we define the problem, what treatment methods to use, and the length of treatment allowed.

For clients presenting with distinct issues (e.g., a conflict in one aspect of life), paradigms for treatment are fairly easily found. A Chinese American woman dealing with internalized racism may enter treatment to work on depression. A White gay man dealing with identity development may enter treatment to work on anxiety associated with the coming out process. But which clinical approach do we use with clients dealing with multiple sources of oppression such as Black lesbians, gay Latinos, and bisexual Korean American men and women? This is a complex clinical concern requiring multiple considerations.

The setting is another major consideration in service delivery. Whether we work in agencies, group or individual private practices, there are policies, guidelines, rules and regulations that determine practical issues such as fees, hours, client selection, treatment selection, and length of treatment. These practical issues interact with clinical issues at the first point of entry of a client connection with a therapist. This interaction thus influences problem definition, approach, and focus of treatment.

In the psychological literature there are numerous works published with respect to clinical issues with people of color (Ponterotto, Casas, Suzuki, & Alexander, 1995; Sue & Sue, 1990), lesbian/gay/bisexuals (Alexander, 1996; Greene & Herek, 1994), and a growing body of literature with respect to lesbians and gay men of color (Greene, 1994a; Morales, 1990). However, a literature search conducted on PsycLit with respect to the interaction of race/ethnicity, gender, sexual orientation, and setting (private practice versus agency) yielded no results.

This finding raises the main question of focus for this article: What is the interaction between the clinical issues and the practical issues (setting) in counseling lesbians and gay men of color in private practice? Since there are no published reports in this area, I will attempt to review major points from each of the areas noted above and supplement with anecdotes from clinical practice as well as discussions with colleagues who work with this population. Therefore the following is a discussion of *considerations* and not absolute, either-or, right-wrong perspectives.

CLINICAL CONSIDERATIONS

Identity Development

A significant body of literature has been developed with respect to issues of identity development for African American gay men (Icard, 1986, Loiacano, 1989), Asian American gay men and lesbians (Chan, 1989; Liu & Chan, 1996; Wooden, Kawasaki, & Mayeda, 1983), Latina lesbians (Espín, 1987), gay Latinos/Latinas (Morales, 1992; Rodriguez, 1996). A recurring theme in these studies is that lesbians and gay men of color express a need to find validation in each community (ethnic and gay/lesbian) and a need to integrate both cultural identities. The "Pull" is another common theme whereby a person feels that he/she must choose between one aspect of identity over the other, resulting in significant levels of confusion, anxiety, and depression.

Rodriguez (1991) examined the process of identity formation in gay Latino men in a qualitative study, interviewing participants about their experiences in developing a gay Latino identity. Developmental issues discussed include: family as the basis for socialization, social class, religion/spirituality, machismo, gender role socialization, not being brown enough/acculturation, language, *familismo*, family dynamics and coming out, socializing in multiple worlds, dating partners, survivors of childhood sexual abuse, HIV/AIDS, and redefinition of *familia*. The issues discussed are offered as clinical questions, assessment markers of identity development, and considerations for clinical intervention with this population.

Morales (1990) presented a model of identity development for ethnic gays and lesbians. Rather than employ the term "stages," he proposed five "states" experienced by gays and lesbians of color: (1) Denial of Conflicts, (2) Bisexual versus Gay/lesbian, (3) Conflicts in Allegiances, (4) Establishing Priorities in Allegiances, and (5) Integrating the Various Communities. Each state describes processes for managing anxiety and tensions. As a person experiences cognitive and behavioral changes, there is a tendency for greater understanding of self (ethnicity and sexual orientation).

Language Issues

The power that words and language possess cannot be over-emphasized. Content, meaning, and affect are all mediated by the words one uses. The language of one culture may or may not easily translate into the culture of another (e.g., gay/lesbian). I recall a Chinese American man explaining how he tried to come out to his mother without the term existing in Chinese. "I tried to tell her that I *love men*. She said, 'Fine, as long as you marry a woman.' " Several authors have noted the presence of negative, but not positive, terms for gay in the Spanish language (Carballo-Diéguez, 1989; Rodriguez, 1996).

With respect to bilingual clients, the choice (conscious or unconscious) of language used to discuss certain issues is important. Several authors have noted that often bilingual clients will split off verbalized experience from emotional experience depending upon which language is being used. Bilingual people may spontaneously switch to the primary language in order to better express what they are experiencing. Sometimes they choose to speak in the secondary language in order to avoid the stress provoked by emotionally charged material (Atkinson, Morten, and Sue, 1989; Falicov, 1982; Parés-Avila and Montano-López, 1994).

In Espín's (1994) research with Latina lesbian immigrants and Liu and Chan's (1996) research with East Asian lesbians and gay men, instances were noted of people talking about their sexuality in English (second language), even though the researchers were bilingual/bicultural. English provided a safe, emotional distance from discussing issues of sexuality which are not culturally sanctioned. The issue for the bilingual/bicultural therapist is to be aware of when use of primary and secondary language may be a clue to a hot emotional topic for the client.

Culturally Proscribed Gender Roles

Each culture has its own set of gender role expectations and sanctions for violation of the roles. Liu and Chan (1996) stated:

> In the family, women are expected to be domestic and family-centered, nurturing, and submissive to males; men are expected to be stoic, strong, and dominant. The ideal is a very tightly knit extended family, with two parents who are both morally principled and dedicated to their families, are not openly affectionate, and are clear about communicating rules and enforcing discipline among children. (p. 138)

From Greene's (1994a) perspective, gender roles in African American families have more flexibility than other ethnic groups due, in part, to a high value on interdependence, egalitarianism, and the need to adapt to racism in the United States. Greene further noted that sexism does, in fact, exist within the African American community, but that family and community functions as a protective barrier and survival tool against racism.

Gender roles are also inextricably intertwined with sexuality. Boykin (1996) discussed what he called the "antilesbian strand of homophobia" that sees woman-woman relationships as threatening to the "ever-important" black family. Lesbians threaten the social structure of the family because they are not viewed as child-bearers, which is the primary mode by which women define their "womanness."

Williams (1992) examined the definition and meaning of sexual orientation in various American Indian cultures, primarily the Lakota Indians. Sexual orientation is defined more in terms of gender categories–femininity and masculinity. In some cultures, certain men are labeled as *berdache* and are viewed as a third sex. In the community, they hold roles of respect and are attributed such characteristics as generosity, spirituality, androgyny, preference for doing women's work, and a preference for having sex with men.

Carballo-Diéguez (1995) interviewed 182 Puerto Rican men who have sex with men (MSM). There were four categories identified by the men: (1) Straight (*hombre*–inserter, do not kiss/fondle the other;

sex with feminine, passive men), (2) Bisexual (*hombres moder-nos*–modern men–engage in more versatile sex; kiss/fondle others), (3) Gay (*entendidos*–those who understand–versatile; prefer sex with men, comfortable with sharing emotions/affection), and (4) Drag Queen (identify, act, live in feminine way and refer to selves as women). He found that for all types, the issue of masculinity and femininity played an important role in how they defined their sexual orientation.

Morales (1996) reviewed the literature on gender roles among Latino gay/bisexual men. He noted from the outset that the role of gender is central to the Spanish language in that gender is assigned not only to living beings, but to inanimate objects–everything in the world is either male or female. Given this backdrop, gender roles become central to the lives of Latinos/Latinas, straight, bisexual, or gay/lesbian.

The running thread through these studies is that homosexuality is viewed from within each of the ethnic cultures as a rejection of proscribed gender roles. Given that gender roles directly relate to cultural identification, to come out as gay/lesbian is viewed as a rejection of the culture. For Latinos, machismo is rejected. For Asians, womanhood is rejected. For Black men, propagation of the family, race, and culture is rejected. Homophobia is the likely end result of these conflicts with the notion that gays are alien and/or inferior (Greene, 1994a; Morales, 1996).

Disclosure/Coming Out

Coming out to significant others is considered a significant event in gay/lesbian identity development (Cass, 1979; Coleman, 1982). These models, however, appear to reflect more the developmental patterns of Caucasian Americans. In her review of the literature of mental health and treatment issues with lesbians and gay men of color, Greene (1994a) examined the meaning of coming out and potential cultural conflicts from diverse ethnic perspectives.

From a Latin American perspective, coming out violates one of the primary cultural values, that of being indirect as the proscribed way of managing conflict. Coming out is then seen as an overt confrontation in terms of forcing the issue and potentially causing the family to lose face.

One of the most salient features of Asian American families is the expectation of obedience to parents and demand for conformity–respect for elders and sharp delineation of gender roles. Coming out is seen as threatening the continuation of the family line and rejection of appropriate roles within the culture.

Given the acknowledged homophobia within the African American community, rejection by family, community, and the church are realistic consequences. Greene (1994a) noted the sense of conflicting loyalties felt by Black lesbians and gay men when confronted by homophobia in the African American community. She further noted that there was a greater likelihood of lesbian/gay African Americans to experience tension and loneliness, but not seek out help.

Native American lesbians and gay men may feel more pressure to be closeted if they live on reservations as a result of internalized oppression/racism and the real or perceived loss of contact with traditional values. The other major influence on homophobia/pressure to remain closeted is the history of colonization and introduction of Christianity to native peoples.

Greene (1994a) further advised clinicians to be wary of the potential misattribution of pathology for the understandable stress resulting from managing multiple oppressions. Clients must be able to maintain ties to their ethnic communities. Coming out, as noted above, could result in rejection by, estrangement, and/or taken as an overt rejection of the community by the individual.

Religion/Spirituality

It is extremely important to assess the degree to which a religious/ spiritual upbringing from a particular culture has affected a person's sense of identity. Within Latino culture, Catholicism remains a strong influence. Many clients have commented, "You can't separate Catholicism from being Chicano–they're one and the same thing." For African Americans, the role of the Black Church is central to family life. From Boykin's (1996) perspective, the significance of the church within the Black community is so powerful that many blacks "dare not stray from it." Liu and Chan (1996) documented the role of 3 major forces–Confucianism, Taoism, and Buddhism–that coexist in a curious mixture in East Asian societies and shape the nature of relationships within the family. Aspects of each have been found to be in conflict with homosexuality.

Whether it be religion, folk beliefs, or other practices, it is important to include a client's sense of spirituality in the overall assessment of his/her issues and in the development of appropriate treatment interventions. A client may or may not currently practice these beliefs, but may still hold them as significant influences on how he/she perceives him/herself in relation to family, culture, society, and the universe. In the studies reviewed for this article, it is interesting to note that while religion was mentioned as influences on homophobia, many lesbian/ gay people of color report that spirituality–faith in God, Goddess, Higher Power–is what buoyed them through the hardships of life (Boykin, 1996; Greene, 1994a; Rodriguez, 1996).

Acculturation/Multiple Identities/Multiple Sources of Oppression

It would be easy for clinicians to interpret all of the cultural norms, values, and beliefs noted above to be absolutes in terms of how they impact a lesbian/gay person of color. This is not always true. The level of acculturation (learning and adopting the characteristics, attitudes, values and beliefs of another culture) must be considered when developing clinical interventions for clients. The "pull" of conflicting loyalties may very well be mediated by acculturation and the client's ties to the ethnic specific values and belief systems.

In Carballo-Diéguez' (1995) study with Puerto Rican men and in Liu and Chan's (1996) review of Lesbian/Gay/Bisexual East Asian Americans, those who openly identified as lesbian/gay were more likely to be highly acculturated and to have been more influenced by American/Western culture. Liu and Chan offered questions to be considered when working with this population that include: Are the client and his or her family members immigrants or American born? What are the specific cultural values of this ethnic group, the client's family members, of the client? How strongly do the client and other family members follow traditional customs (p. 145)?

In many cultures, homosexuality is viewed as a "White man's disease," thus promoting the invisibility of lesbian and gay men of color in society (Tremble, Schneider, & Appathurai, 1989). It is often stated that when a person of color comes out, that he/she has been "hanging around with the White people too long." In my clinical experience, that attitude becomes a significant contributing factor to internalized racism and homophobia in that it sends the message that they are not ethnic "enough" and that by being gay/lesbian, they have turned their back on their community. Sexuality is considered an invisible minority status while race/ethnicity is a visible minority status.

How could one possibly risk being rejected by their ethnic community (the primary source for emotional/physical/spiritual support against White racism) by coming out? The invisible status could also be interpreted as privilege in that "You can pass as straight, but not as White." The attitude also sends the message that members of their own ethnic community are potential sources of threat and stress who will reject and ostracize them for not conforming. It would be easy to generalize this fear to the entire culture, thereby making the ethnic aspect of their identity something to be feared and hated.

Lesbians and gay men of color are faced with managing life in three different worlds: the ethnic community, the gay/lesbian community, and the predominantly white, heterosexual community (Greene, 1994b; Liu & Chan, 1996; Morales, 1990). Each setting carries with it an emotional either-or, zero-sum "pull," which creates both internal conflict and conflict with the community. Racism exists in the lesbian/gay community just as it does in the heterosexual community. Homophobia exists in the communities of color just as it does in the white community. In today's "check only one box" society, many people from multicultural backgrounds end up as "other."

Lesbians and gay men of color frequently report feeling alone, isolated, alienated–a sense of never being a part of any one group (Greene, 1994a, 1994b; Liu & Chan, 1996; Morales, 1990). These authors document the existence of multiple sources of oppression–racism, sexism, homophobia/heterosexism–which add a significant level of stress for people. Many people feel conflicting loyalties, given that they are double and sometimes triple minority status people, marginalized within each culture.

In their study of the definition and meaning of Chicano ethnicity, Keefe and Padilla (1987) reported that one factor, cultural loyalty, is a function of real or perceived threat. If a Chicana felt that the American side of her was being threatened, she would lean more towards that side for a period of time. When she feels threat more on the Mexican side, she will probably lean towards that side. In Chan's (1989) study, participants chose to identify and ally themselves more closely with the lesbian/gay side or the Asian American side at different times, depending upon need, situational factors, and self-concept.

In 1992, the Governor of California vetoed Assembly Bill 101 which would have added sexual orientation to the non-discrimination policy of the State. Angry protests and demonstrations occurred all over the state, with identifiable lesbian and gay men of color organizations. It can be interpreted that these individuals were, perhaps, leaning towards the lesbian/gay side due to threat/oppression. In 1995, the State of California passed Proposition 187 which was viewed by many as anti-immigrant and racist. Gay and lesbian of color organizations were part of the demonstrations and in so doing, leaned toward the ethnic side due to threat/oppression. Capitalizing on this concept, the phrase that I have found useful with clients is: "It is healthy to lean."

Liu and Chan (1996) acknowledged both the challenges and opportunities inherent in multiple roles and multiple communities. Being a lesbian/gay person of color can be a source of strength and resilience, given the depth and breadth of perspectives on families and life experiences from both cultural identities. "It is easier to shift one's cultural lens when one has been exposed to both East Asian and Western views, allowing for more flexibility and adaptability in interpreting and responding to life events" (p. 145).

A fourth "world" is becoming more and more apparent that acknowledges all aspects of a person's life: the lesbian/gay community of color (Rodriguez, 1996). Reporting on previous research, Rodriguez noted that socializing in the gay Latino community was one of the main support systems that helped participants deal with the "missing" or overlooked cultural parts of themselves. Morales (1996) documented the existence of local, state, and national Latino gay men's organizations which foster further social connection and thus reduce isolation and alienation associated with "the pull." Knowledge of these community resources could be an excellent adjunct intervention to social support.

This concludes the section on clinical considerations. I concur with Greene's (1994a) cautions about making gross generalizations of cultural practices and views and applying them uniformly to all members of an ethnic group. Individual differences exist and it is important that both the therapist and the client be aware of this. For a more detailed review of these issues, including treatment implications, countertransference dilemmas, and mental health dilemmas, refer to Greene (1994a).

PRACTICAL CONSIDERATIONS

Social Class

One of the first items to be considered with respect to engaging in private practice work is that private practice is the *business* of psychotherapy (Barker, 1983). He further noted that prior to World War II, psychotherapy and private practice was considered a luxury–an elitist privilege. From a supply-side economics point of view, as long as the demand for treatment remains, there will be adequate employment for therapists to provide services. The question becomes, who has the economic resources to pay for these services?

The first issue in which clinical interacts with practical is the socioeconomic class of the population for whom practice is being advertised. Although people of color are represented in the various levels of SES, it is documented that the overall income level of people of color is lower than their White counterparts and that the unemployment rate of people of color is higher than their White counterparts (U.S. Department of Commerce, Bureau of the Census, 1989). It is also well-documented that overall, people of color experience more problems accessing both health and mental health care as a result of SES issues. Other contributing factors to these results include scarcity of culturally-relevant service delivery, overt and institutionalized racism, and the cultural-specific norm with respect to counseling/psychotherapy.

The establishment of community-based clinics for specific populations is a direct result of all of the aforementioned issues. Lesbian/Gay/Bisexual Community Services Centers and mental health clinics do exist in many major cities. The question for clients becomes: How White is it and does it really serve the needs of people of color? Likewise, many ethnic-specific agencies exist. For these, the question becomes: How heterosexist/homophobic might it be and does it adequately serve the needs of lesbian/gay/bisexual clients?

For some clients, the lack of a community-based agency which meets their multicultural needs may be a reason to seek out a private practitioner. The drawback to this for people from a lower SES group is that he/she will be paying fees potentially outside of their range. The person may already feel disempowered (clinical considerations section) and may present as hesitant to asking about fees and following through with setting an appointment. If the person is employed, has an adequate salary with adequate health/mental health insurance benefits, the fee may not be so much of a problem.

For therapists whose primary income is their private practice, fees become an important issue–on both a practical and clinical level. Borofsky and Chipman (1982) pointed out a potential conflict for these therapists with respect to seeing clients from lower SES categories. The external economic life of the therapist could affect the therapeutic relationship due to material deprivation, guilt about the therapist's own SES, privilege, and anxiety about cash flow predictability. At the extreme, it is possible that the therapist could place his/her own economic needs above the client's actual clinical needs in terms of frequency and duration of treatment.

Borofsky and Chipman (1982) addressed another potential form of countertransference:

> It may well be then, that therapists invariably reach a stage of crisis in their professional development where the current reality conditions of their professional practice setting is in painful conflict with the internalized ideals derived from their earlier socialization to the practice of psychotherapy. (p. 17)

Training in ethical standards of the practice of psychotherapy for most disciplines usually includes suggestions about performing pro-bono work and/or setting aside slots for low-fee clients. Since private practice is a business, therapists are also forced to consider their own SES level in implementing this aspiration and providing needed services to a population that is underserved. For therapists from a minority group, cultural expectations often dictate a "giving back to the community" attitude. This could also pose a potential conflict, resulting in countertransference issues.

Race, Private Practice, and Cross Cultural Psychotherapy

DeWeaver (1992) examined the correlation between race of therapist and the decision to go into private practice. He sampled a group of private practice social workers in Atlanta and looked at the characteristics of 70 social workers and their effects on private practice. DeWeaver found that Black social workers entered private practice from the onset of acquiring their MSW faster than their White counterparts. Reasons provided for the decision were: autonomy, flexibility, economics, and potential for personal satisfaction. In addition, he found significant differences in terms of Black social workers using private practice as their primary income while their White counterparts used private practice to supplement their income. Although this study did not include sexual orientation as a variable, one could hypothesize about its correlation to lesbian/gay therapists of color and to the aforementioned potential problematic countertransference issues with regard to the SES of both therapist and client.

It is important for the therapist to note the potential negative transference feelings a lesbian/gay client of color may have for an ethnic, lesbian/gay, or lesbian/gay of color therapist. Clients in the beginning stages of cultural identity development may fear homophobia from a therapist of color and/or racism from a lesbian/gay Anglo therapist. As noted in Helms (1993), counseling impasses often occur in situations when the counselor and the client are at significantly different stages of racial identity development. A client in a devaluation stage of ethnicity and/or sexual orientation may not trust or have interest seeing an identified ethnically, lesbian/gay, or lesbian/gay therapist of color.

As Atkinson, Morten, and Sue (1989) concluded, counselor-client cultural differences alone do not create barriers to counseling. A therapist's sensitivity to and knowledge of critical aspects of multicultural issues in therapy will influence his/her ability to work effectively with a lesbian/gay client of color. Providing services to this population can be considered a clinical specialty. Hence, any therapist of any sexual orientation and any race/ethnicity and any social class can effectively work with this population as long as he/she has training and experience in the clinical and practical issues.

Referral Sources

In the business of psychotherapy, private practitioners are also concerned with the market–sources of referral. Another reason for a client seeking private practice services is the reputation and particular level of expertise the practitioner has. Obviously, when a practitioner is known in the community and has built a solid reputation, he/she is more likely to receive referrals. Morrison (1983) tracked referral sources of his practice over a five year period. He found that monthly and seasonal fluctuations did not seem to be major factors and that over 50% of his referrals came from current and previous clients.

From Morrison's (1983) perspective, private practice generates most of its own business. There is no mention as to the race/ethnicity of the author nor of his clients. Given that his practice could be considered rural (population approximately 500,000 in up-state New York), one could hypothesize that the "small-town feel" of the author's practice could relate to the "small-town feel" of lesbians and gay men of color (minority within a minority).

Boundary Issues

Given the small community perspective inherent in providing services to this population, boundary issues become an even more salient issue for the private practitioner. Gartrell (1994) examined boundaries in lesbian therapist-client relationships. She identified several areas for consideration, including: (1) level and amount of appropriate self-disclosure, (2) appropriateness of physical contact and risk for sexual exploitation, (3) special treatment (giving preferences for low fee/no fee, prime time therapy hours, hugs, payment arrangements), (4) gifts (given and received), (5) personal privacy in the community (therapist has a right to privacy of his/her personal life), and managing relationships with former clients (psychotherapy is a unilateral relationship that carries on beyond termination).

All of these areas can become potentially problematic when we consider how small the community of lesbian/gay people of color is. Lesbians and gays of color play multiple roles regardless of being a therapist or a client: family member, community member, social/political activist, teacher, student, and consultant. And in the context of each role, we all have needs. I concur with Gartrell's (1994) suggestion that therapists utilize peer consultation/supervision. In this way, therapists can have their social, political, and professional needs met through connection with their peers rather than utilizing their contact with clients for this purpose.

Consultation can also prove incredibly useful when dealing with real-life boundary issues such as having an initial session with a client who is the former partner of a current/former client seen during the break-up, or being in social, political, or religious settings in which the client also participates. Although boundary issues apply to all therapists (agency and private practice), this issue can become an even more restrictive pressure when the therapist, client, or both are members of a small community. This pressure affects the therapeutic relationship and therefore is an issue worth exploring.

CONCLUSION

In this article I have attempted to merge both clinical and practical considerations in providing services to lesbians and gay men of color in a private practice setting. Issues such as level of identity development, language usage, definition and meaning of coming out, religion/ spirituality, and acculturation/multiple sources of oppression are constantly interacting with issues of social class of both the client and therapist, race and sexual orientation of the therapist, referral sources, and boundary issues in a small community–diversity within a diverse community.

Knowledge of other community resources is also extremely important. Given the emotional and moral support available from identified lesbian/gay individuals of color and organizations, it is important for the therapist to introduce these sources of support when the client indicates that he/she is ready to investigate this realm. Once the client begins to develop a support system and establishes his/her new family (those who love and support him/her for who he/she is), it would be helpful for the therapist to affirm and validate the function of redefined family in the person's life.

We do not operate in a vacuum; nor do our clients. The more that we can support a community-oriented perspective (however defined by the person), the more we become promoters of culturally-relevant perspectives that fit the worldviews of our clients, our colleagues, and ourselves.

REFERENCES

Alexander, C. (editor) (1996). *Gay and lesbian mental health: A source book for practitioners*. New York, NY: Harrington Park Press.

Atkinson, D.R., Morten, G., & Sue, D.W. (1989). *Counseling American minorities*. (3rd ed.). Dubuque, IA: William C. Brown Publishers.

Barker, R.L. (1983). Supply side economics in private psychotherapy practice: Some ominous and encouraging trends. *Psychotherapy in Private Practice*, *1*(1), pp. 71-82.

Borofsky, G.L., & Chipman, A. (1982). A contextual schema for privately and publicly practiced psychotherapy. *Psychotherapy: Theory, Research and Practice*, *19*(1), pp. 9-17.

Boykin, K. (1996). *One more river to cross: Black and gay in America*. New York, NY: Anchor Books, Doubleday.

Carballo-Diéguez, A. (1995). The sexual identity and behavior of Puerto Rican men who have sex with men. In G.M. Herek and B. Greene (eds.) *AIDS, identity, and community: The HIV epidemic and lesbians and gay men* (pp. 105-114). Thousand Oaks, CA: Sage Publications.

Carballo-Diéguez, A. (1989). Hispanic culture, gay male culture, and AIDS: Counseling implications. *Journal of Counseling & Development, 68*(September/October), 26-30.

Cass, V.C. (1979). Homosexual identity formation: A theoretical model. *Journal of Homosexuality, 4*(3), 219-235.

Chan, C.S. (1989). Issues of identity development among Asian-American lesbians and gay men. *Journal of Counseling & Development, 68*(September/October), 16-20.

Coleman, E. (1982). Developmental stages of the coming out process. *Journal of Homosexuality, 7*, 31-43.

DeWeaver, K.L. (1992). Race, private practice, and psychotherapy: An empirical examination and discussion. *Psychotherapy in Private Practice, 11*(1), pp. 49-67.

Espín, O. (1994). Crossing borders and boundaries: The life narratives of immigrant lesbians. Symposium at the annual convention of the American Psychological Association, Los Angeles, CA.

Espín, O.M. (1987). Issues of identity in the psychology of Latina lesbians. In Boston Lesbians Psychologies Collective (Eds.), *Lesbian psychologies* (pp. 35-51). Urbana: University of Illinois Press.

Falicov, C.J. (1982). Mexican families. In M. McGoldrick, J.K. Pearce, & J. Giordano (eds.) *Ethnicity & family therapy* (pp. 134-163). New York, NY: The Guilford Press.

Gartrell, N.K. (1994). Boundaries in lesbian therapist-client relationships. In B. Greene & G.J. Herek (eds.). *Lesbian and gay psychology: Theory, research, and clinical applications*. Thousand Oaks, CA: Sage Publications.

Greene, B. (1994a). Ethnic-minority lesbians and gay men: Mental health and treatment issues. *Journal of Consulting and Clinical Psychology, 62*(2), pp. 243-251.

Greene, B. (1994b). Lesbian women of color: Triple jeopardy. In Comas-Diaz, L. & Greene, B. (eds.) *Women of color: Integrating ethnic and gender identities in psychotherapy* (pp. 389-427). New York, NY: Guilford Press.

Greene, B., & Herek, G.M. (Eds.) (1994). *Lesbian and gay psychology: Theory, research, and clinical applications*. Thousand Oaks, CA: Sage Publications.

Helms, J. (1993). *Black and white racial identity: Theory, research, and practice*. New York: Greenwood Press.

Icard, L. (1986). Black gay men and conflicting social identities: Sexual orientation versus racial identity. In J. Gripton & M. Valentich (Eds.), [Special issue of the *Journal of Social Work & Human Sexuality, 4*(1/2)]. *Social work practice in sexual problems*, 83-93. New York: The Haworth Press, Inc.

Keefe, S.E., & Padilla, A. (1987). *Chicano ethnicity*. Albuquerque, NM: University of New Mexico Press.

Liu, P., & Chan, C. (1996). Lesbian, gay, and bisexual Asian Americans and their families. In J. Laird and R. Jay-Green (eds.) *Lesbians and gays in couples and families* (pp. 137-152). San Francisco, CA: Jossey-Bass Publishers.

Loiacano, D.K. (1989). Gay identity issues among Black Americans: Racism, homophobia, and the need for validation. *Journal of Counseling & Development, 68*(September/October), 21-25.

Morales, E.S. (1996). Gender roles among Latino gay and bisexual men. In J. Laird and R. Jay-Green (Eds.), *Lesbians and gays in couples and families* (pp. 272-297). San Francisco, CA: Jossey-Bass Publishing.

Morales, E.S. (1992). Counseling Latino gays and Latina lesbians. In S.H. Dworkin & F.J. Gutierrez (Eds.) *Counseling gay men & lesbians: Journey to the end of the rainbow.* Alexandria, VA: American Counseling Association (pp. 125-139).

Morales, E.S. (1990). Ethnic minority families and minority gays and lesbians. In F.W. Bozett & M.B. Sussman (Eds.), *Homosexuality and family relations* (pp. 217-239). New York: The Haworth Press, Inc.

Morrison, J.K. (1983). Tracking referrals for psychotherapy in private practice: The first five years. *Psychotherapy in Private Practice, 1*(4), pp. 9-14.

Parés-Avila, J.A., & Montano-López, R.M. (1994). Issues in the psychosocial care of Latino gay men with HIV infection. In S.A. Cadwell, R.A. Burham, & M. Forstein (Eds.), *Therapists on the front line: Psychotherapy with gay men in the age of AIDS.* Washington, D.C.: American Psychiatric Press, Inc. (pp. 339-362).

Ponterotto, J.G., Casas, J.M., Suzuki, L.A., & Alexander, C.M. (Eds.) (1995). *Handbook of multicultural counseling.* Thousand Oaks, CA: Sage Publications.

Rodriguez, R.A. (1996). Clinical issues in identity development in gay Latino men. In C.J. Alexander (Ed.), *Gay and lesbian mental health: A sourcebook for practitioners* (pp. 127-157). New York, NY: Harrington Park Press.

Rodriguez, R.A. (1991). *A qualitative study of identity development in gay Chicano men.* Unpublished doctoral dissertation, University of Utah, Salt Lake City, Utah.

Sue, D.W., & Sue, D. (1990). *Counseling the culturally different (2nd ed).* New York, NY: John Wiley & Sons Publishers.

Tremble, B., Schneider, M., & Appathurai, C. (1989). Growing up gay or lesbian in a multicultural context. In G. Herdt (Ed.), *Gay and lesbian youth* (pp. 253-267). New York, NY: The Haworth Press, Inc.

United States Department of Commerce (1989). *Census Report.* Washington, D.C: United States of America.

Williams, W. (1992). *The spirit and the flesh: Sexual diversity in American Indian culture.* Boston, MA: Beacon Press.

Wooden, W.S., Kawasaki, H., & Mayeda, R. (1983). Lifestyles and identity maintenance among gay Japanese-American males. *Alternative Lifestyles, 5,* 236-243.

Boundary Issues in Gay and Lesbian Psychotherapy Relationships

Jim Fickey
Gary Grimm

SUMMARY. Gay and lesbian psychotherapists face unique challenges when working with clients who also identify as gay or lesbian. Of particular importance are the roles professional boundaries play in working with sexual minorities. For example, clinicians must decide whether it is in the client's best interests to know the therapist is gay. Issues of contact outside of the therapy hour also become important, particularly when the therapist lives in a small community, or otherwise risks the possibility of seeing the client in the community. This chapter addresses some of these issues, and poses options for therapists on how to minimize professional boundary or ethical violations. *[Article copies available for a fee from The Haworth Document Delivery Service: 1-800-342-9678. E-mail address: getinfo@haworthpressinc.com]*

All major mental health professions have prohibitions against any type of relationship that will impair the therapist's ability to function in an ethical, professional and therapeutic manner. Most of the literature that deals with ethics within the psychotherapeutic community is very consistent when it addresses the issue of boundaries:

> Dual relationships with clients that might impair the member's objectivity and professional judgment (e.g., as with close friends or relatives, sexual intimacies with any client) must be avoided

---

Jim Fickey, MS, and Gary Grimm, MS, are in private practice in Santa Fe, NM.

[Haworth co-indexing entry note]: "Boundary Issues in Gay and Lesbian Psychotherapy Relationships." Fickey, Jim and Gary Grimm. Co-published simultaneously in *Journal of Gay & Lesbian Social Services* (The Haworth Press, Inc.) Vol. 8, No. 4, 1998, pp. 77-93; and: *Working with Gay Men and Lesbians in Private Psychotherapy Practice* (ed: Christopher J. Alexander) The Haworth Press, Inc., 1998, pp. 77-93. Single or multiple copies of this article are available for a fee from The Haworth Document Delivery Service [1-800-342-9678, 9:00 a.m. - 5:00 p.m. (EST). E-mail address: getinfo@haworthpressinc.com].

and/or the counseling relationship terminated through referral to another competent professional. (AACD, 1981, in Corey, 1985, p. 32)

These codes typically caution against attempting to establish social or personal relationships with clients under any circumstances. What we, as gay and lesbian psychotherapists, need to address is whether strict adherence to the traditional model of roles and boundaries works. The prohibition against sexual contact between therapist and client is indisputable. That is, it is a boundary to which the therapist must strictly adhere. However, we challenge some of the other existing boundary rules in order to address the specific needs of the gay therapist and client. In short, how can the gay therapist ease the rules concerning acceptable boundary maintenance, such as fraternization outside the therapy office, and still behave professionally and ethically?

Heyward (1994) attempts to address some of these issues. She believes that many of the lines that separate professional and peer relationships are artificial and debilitating. She stresses that rules that are applied by professional organizations do not keep clients safe and that much abuse has been done by professionals well-known for their clear boundaries.

Another position is expressed by Green (1996) in her article, "When a Therapist Breaks the Rules." She tells the story of her experience with a therapist who clearly violated the rules of professional behavior, thus demonstrating how one should not cross boundaries. There will always be therapists who cannot adhere to ethical principles of psychotherapy and will tend to break the rules and the law.

CHALLENGES GAY THERAPISTS FACE COMING OUT

Coming out is an essential element in the process of healing from the stigma of being gay. How then can gay therapists effectively work with gay clients, while at the same time continuing their own process of coming out? One option is to come out to the client. Contrary to the traditional psychoanalytic model, where the therapist discloses little, if anything, about him or herself, a more humanistic model includes coming out to the client. In this way, the therapist serves as a positive role model providing the gay client with much-needed support. In the article, "The Gay Male Therapist as an Agent of Socialization," Kooden (1994) addresses the issue of therapists as positive role models:

> By definition, in a healthy relationship, projections are minimal. Thus, the more the therapist-client relationship is based on positive, present interaction and the less it is based on projection and transference, the closer the client will move towards experiencing himself as a strong person. (p. 50)

Although there are many gay therapists today who withhold their sexual orientation from gay clients, we believe it imperative that gay therapists be out to their clients. Kooden's position, although not specifically geared toward the issue of coming out, clearly supports such a disclosure as a means of strengthening the therapist/client relationship.

Further, when a gay therapist withholds his sexual orientation from a gay client, we question to what extent such withholding can actually damage the therapeutic relationship by creating distance or confusion for the client. Further, questions are raised about to what extent withholding one's sexual orientation could indicate unresolved, internalized homophobia within the therapist. Although the literature seems to suggest that knowledge of the therapist's sexual orientation does not affect the client's satisfaction with or expectations about therapy, internalized homophobia does impact the client's success within the therapeutic process (Lease, Cogdal, & Smith, 1995).

Therapeutic boundaries inevitably change when the therapist comes out to the client. By the very nature of coming out, the therapist, for a brief moment in time, enters into a peer dynamic with the client. This disclosure reveals to the client something the two have in common. That is, the therapist is communicating, In this way, I am like you. Such a departure from the normal therapist/client dynamic, which includes a certain degree of inequity or dissimilarity, can offer the client a feeling of empowerment and camaraderie with the therapist. As Kooden (1994) points out, "This is consistent with the therapist as a positive role model, of practicing what he is teaching" (p. 51).

Despite the overwhelming positive reasons for gay therapists to be out to their gay clients, there are also potential negative outcomes. Depending on the client's level of internalized homophobia, he or she could project on to the therapist their own feelings of self-hatred, thereby lessening the potential benefits of working with a gay therapist. Therefore, it is possible that a gay client's homophobia could negatively impact the therapeutic process when he or she knows of the therapist's sexual orientation (Schwartz, 1989).

How and when therapists come out to gay clients, and in what setting, is also of particular importance. We believe that with most high-functioning gay clients, such a disclosure can be done as early as the first session. Of course, there are exceptions to this. With clients who suffer from severe (and unacknowledged) internalized homophobia, such a disclosure could result in a premature and hasty termination.

Also, coming out early in the therapeutic process allows the therapist to set the stage for an open, honest and direct communication between himself and the client. This can be done casually and without fanfare. For example, we will sometimes say, "One of the things I'd like you to know about me is that I'm a gay man and have been in a relationship with a man for many years. Do you have any questions you'd like to ask me about this? How do you feel knowing more about who I am?"

Such a disclosure is most successfully incorporated into the client's work if it happens inside the therapy office. Clients who discover outside the therapy office that the therapist is gay (e.g., running into them at the local gay bar) may feel a tremendous sense of betrayal. In turn, clients may develop legitimate concerns about trust, and rightfully question to what extent they can believe in a therapist who has withheld such an essential part of himself.

Involvement in the gay community, both socially and politically, may be as important for the therapist as it is for the client. Kooden (1994) writes, "I believe that involvement and participation in the world beyond one's front door are an essential component of mental health" (p. 50). He further explains:

> If the therapist believes that his inherent power can be successfully expressed in social activism and that social activism is a component of mental health, then it is best if the therapist is involved in some form of community participation. (p. 51)

The needs of the therapist to continue his own coming out process should not be overlooked. This may be addressed in a variety of ways, such as becoming involved in social and political activities. In doing so, he or she understands that they may run into or even engage in interaction with one or more of their clients.

As mentioned elsewhere in this chapter, the extent of engagement or interaction outside the therapy office must be determined by the therapist, and if, at any time, he or she begins to feel compromised or perceive that such interaction could jeopardize the therapeutic relationship, such a process would need to cease. However, this possibility should not prevent the therapist from doing some of what he or she must do to affirm their own sexual identity. They simply need to be cautious and use common sense and remember to keep the best interest of the client in the forefront.

THERAPISTS IN SMALL TOWNS

As a rule of thumb, the smaller the community, the greater the chance that the therapist and client will cross paths outside the office. In small towns, seeing clients in the community becomes just a matter of time. In our experience, when clients see us outside the therapy office (especially when we are seen together) they will often need to discuss this in their next therapy session. As a result, we suggest that therapists ask clients in the following session (no matter how incidental or brief the incident may have seemed) if discussing the topic would be helpful. In our experience, it is not uncommon for the client, at first, to minimize the importance of such a question, only to return to it later in the same session.

Issues of confidentiality are often triggered in clients who see their therapist in another context. Clients who see their therapist outside of therapy need reassurance that we are maintaining our agreement of absolute confidentiality. In our experience, clients periodically express their appreciation for our ability to maintain professional boundaries and confidentiality. Such expression may also serve to remind the therapist of the importance of this commitment. This, of course, is one of the best methods of establishing trust: demonstrating through behavior, your ability to maintain a confidential relationship.

Another issue facing therapists in small towns is knowing other people in the client's life. Some of the people clients talk about may even be other clients. Given the possibility of such a situation occurring, it is extremely important that therapists be able to maintain a position of neutrality when clients speaks of mutual acquaintances. Kitchener (1988) writes:

> Professionals who work in small communities may similarly be unable to avoid playing two roles with a client. While this author knows of no studies surveying the ethical dilemmas of mental health professionals who practice in rural areas, a recent survey of rural physicians (Purtilo & Sorrell, 1986) identified the overlapping of professional and personal relationships as one of the major ethical issues that they faced. (p. 220)

What are precautionary measures therapists can take to manage the impact of outside contact with clients? First, as written earlier, it is important to discuss with clients that outside encounters, however brief or seemingly incidental, will need to be discussed. Such encounters often prove to be of profound significance to the client. Within such encounters, the client is offered a view of the therapist in a new and different context. This can help the client to develop a more multi-dimensional view of his therapist–namely, as a more authentic human being.

In a study conducted by Salisbury and Kinnier (1996), they write: "It is clear that the primary concern of counselors is the potential of harm to clients, which is a major tenet of the ethical code" (p. 499). We agree that this should be the primary concern at all times and that therapists must be ever-vigilant to the potential for harm to the client. However, as gay therapists model behavior of responsible adults, we cannot simply rely on rules of conduct, but must increasingly use our intuitive strengths to set appropriate boundaries.

Another primary challenge that therapists who practice in small towns can face is in feeling a heightened sense of loneliness and isolation, conditions all too familiar to many gay men. In such a case, if the therapist fails to acknowledge such feelings, his ability to maintain healthy boundaries with his client may become impaired. If he lacks an adequate support network in meeting his intellectual, emotional and spiritual needs, he may inadvertently attempt to get some or all of these needs met within the context of his professional role. The small town gay therapist must therefore closely monitor and assess his or her degree of loneliness and isolation, and seek appropriate assistance with such situations.

COUNTERTRANSFERENCE

Cadwell (1994) explores several issues related to countertransference that are of particular concern to gay and lesbian therapists. He believes that anger, over-identification, and internalized homophobia are particularly noteworthy. Certainly gay therapists are as susceptible to homophobia as are their clients, as the oppression and stigmatization of gays by society is the same for the therapist as it is for the client. Lima et al. (1993) write: "In pursuit of their identity, gay males [therapist and client] must continually confront societal belief systems which strongly contradict the value of their personhood" (p. 74). Thus, it is of utmost importance that the gay therapist continually address his own issues of internalized homophobia.

How do therapists manage their anger or the pull to over-identify, since so many of these characteristics match our clients'? Therapists may unwittingly avoid expressing strong feelings or exploring certain areas for fear of causing the client undue discomfort because of over-identification with his client's issues. Most research done in this area pertains to female therapists' countertransference toward female clients. Cadwell (1994) writes, "Ruderman [1986] suggests that feelings that derive from society's negative attitude toward women become activated in a female psychotherapist's countertransference, leading to powerful and complex identification with the patient" (p. 83). This same process occurs for the gay therapist and must be explored and monitored. This over-identification can trigger the therapist's own anger concerning feelings of victimization and societal marginalization and result in the therapist's impotence as an agent of change for the client.

OVERIDENTIFICATION WITH AIDS CLIENTS

Another boundary issue that warrants further attention and research, particularly for gay male therapists, concerns the therapists' work with gay men with HIV, especially those with an AIDS diagnosis. Many factors can affect boundaries within such a situation: the therapist's own HIV status, the number of people he has already lost (including lovers, clients, friends, etc.), the extent to which he has grieved these losses, his personal views regarding death, etc. In Steven Cadwell's (1994) study, he reported:

> Therapists described losing perspective because of too much intimacy or too much distance; boundaries lost or never approached. Therapists talked of being over-protective and too active at times. A therapist whose lover had died of AIDS told about being confronted by his client after the therapist had been unusually active in cautioning him against getting involved with a man who was HIV-positive, even though they were practicing safer sex and the relationship had promise. (p. 88)

There are times when the therapist might be asked to visit the client in the hospital or at the client's home. While most therapists would agree that out-of-office sessions would be acceptable under such circumstances, because of their potential frequency and emotional intensity, such sessions could challenge the therapist to readjust his sense of boundaries. This is especially true with a client who is in the final stages of the disease. In these instances, it may not be as necessary to maintain such a professional distance. Instead the client may want and need more touch and physical closeness. We believe as long as such touch is appropriate and non-sexual, it can serve as comfort for the client in a time of potential loneliness and fear. Clearly, this is an example where relaxing a therapeutic boundary can be the most ethical response to an extraordinary situation.

Potentially, another consequence of dealing with clients who may be dying is the therapists' own expression of strong emotions. Traditionally, therapists are expected to control their feelings in the therapeutic setting. Emotions that are directed toward the client would be included in issues of countertransference. But quite often, therapists have worked for an extended period with a particular client and have formed a strong attachment to this person. It would not only be unnatural for the therapist to show no emotion as he or she watches the decline of the client, but inherently dishonest.

It is not the display of emotions that is potentially problematic, but rather, the lack of understanding between therapist and client about how to handle these emotions. It is quite possible that the client will initially feel a need to care for or rescue the therapist. This is a burden the client is ill-equipped to handle at such a time in his life. One of our terminally ill clients did not want his mother to visit him as he neared death for just this reason. He did not have the strength or energy to address his mother's sadness and fear, therefore having to comfort her.

What must be made clear to clients is that the therapist will be responsible for his or her own feelings. When a client of the authors, we'll call him Carl, was very near death, he wanted to talk about the possibility of suicide, should he become incapacitated or develop great pain. This was very hard to hear and I was extremely grief-stricken. As my eyes began to tear, Carl looked at me with an expression of great concern and stopped talking. I immediately explained to him that, although it was difficult for me to hear him speak of his possible suicide and imminent death, he did not have to take care of me. I would be responsible for my emotions, that I could handle them, and that I had other sources of support outside our therapy. He was then able to relax and continued exploring the issues surrounding his death and possible suicide. He eventually died with great dignity without committing suicide.

EXPERIENTIAL THERAPY

Particular questions about boundaries can arise when the therapeutic work moves into an experiential domain. Experiential therapy is defined as therapy that uses cooperative games, initiative problem-solving, low- and high-challenge ropes course elements, and other adventure activities (Schoel, Pruty, & Radcliffe, 1996). Almost all experiential work occurs outdoors, sometimes in controlled environments, oftentimes in nature. Kurt Hahn, an educator in Germany before World War II, started a program called Outward Bound. This program was established in the United States in 1962, as Colorado Outward Bound in Marble, Colorado. This was the beginning of challenge courses (ropes courses) and experiential education in this country (Meyers, 1997).

The authors have expanded their work with gay men by offering experiential therapy workshops. Within the context of experiential therapy, therapists often have an opportunity to engage in some of the proscribed activities with the client. It is up to the therapist to determine the degree to which he or she feels comfortable and the extent of their participation in experiential work. Ropes courses can provide an example of this process.

A ropes course may consist of several initiatives (problems the participants must solve as a group), such as how to get the group across an expanse with various constraints placed on their choices.

The point is to make the task as difficult as possible (without making it impossible) in order to facilitate team-building. By doing this, the idea is that individual issues percolate to the forefront.

It may also consist of several climbing elements. Traditionally, these elements are elevated between 20 and 40 feet and consist of different climbing challenges, each increasing in difficulty. One such element is the "climbing wall" used for rock climbing therapy. Even though the climb is perfectly safe (the participants are in a climbing harness, supported by a belay team), the participants may feel as if they are doing something extremely dangerous and threatening. If participants have unresolved trauma from childhood, they will often exhibit a trauma response during the climb (Allen & Edwards, 1997). No one is forced to do anything against their will, and if they become too frightened, they are allowed to climb down. If the client elects to keep climbing, though, they often break free of the paralyzing fear they have lived with most of their life.

Several of our clients have reported that the experience has been life-transforming. One client, for example, left a job he had hated for years and actually applied for a job in another city. Another left an abusive relationship he had wanted to leave for months. Both of these clients felt that participation in the ropes course was the precipitating factor in their ability to change. It helped them to redefine themselves as empowered human beings rather than as victims.

During these courses, we often participate in individual events such as the climbing wall or the courage pole (where participants jump off a 20 foot pole while suspended in mid-air by ropes to which they are harnessed) with the others observing and offering support. At times, our clients are involved in the belay system (the system which insures the safety of the person harnessed, which can occasionally include the therapists). In such a setting, clients have reported feeling a sense of empowerment, knowing that they were helping to provide safety for their therapist, an experience not usually provided in traditional therapy. At other times, we may be a part of the belay team, which can create a powerful, positive transference for the client.

When our clients engage in group activities that deal with team-building and problem-solving (where the participation of the therapist would unduly influence the process, tilt the balance of power, and possibly contaminate group cooperation), we choose to become observers and maintain a certain distance. By setting this boundary, we can participate in other activities of the group without interfering with and complicating their process. Though this type of intervention is therapeutic, it challenges therapists to stay aware of their role and of their ethical responsibilities.

EROS

Regarding the ethics of sexual relationships with clients, the professional codes of the American Psychological Association (APA, 1992) and the American Counseling Association (ACA, 1993) are very clear. Both strictly forbid these types of relationships. The harm done to the client, the therapist and concurrently to the whole therapeutic community when therapists engage sexually with clients has far-reaching consequences (Regehr & Glancy, 1995). We are in complete agreement with these codes, and at no time do we support sexual relationships of any type with clients.

However, at some point in the therapist's practice, he or she may encounter a client to whom they are sexually attracted. In such a situation, when "eros" is present in the therapeutic process, most schools of psychotherapy recommend that the therapist terminate, or at best, time-limit his work with the client. Such philosophies assume that the therapist may be ill-equipped to deal with their own countertransference, which could limit their effectiveness, decrease their ability to be objective, and in time, take both the therapist and his client into dangerous realms. Although this may be true for some therapists, it is not true for all. With eros present, therapist and client are offered an opportunity to experience a deeper connection, and a sense of sacredness within the work.

Thus, the therapist must possess an ability not to act out his desires or fantasies toward the client. Working effectively with a client when eros is present takes great skill. Though not easy, when accomplished, the client will feel a greater sense of positive regard and appreciation for the therapist. It can yield considerable rewards for the therapist as well, providing the therapist with an opportunity to explore and heal their own narcissistic tendencies. In turn, they can deepen their understanding of unattainable desire, or more simply, of not getting that which they desire. This becomes a powerful lesson for us all as gay men and lesbians.

Also, this can be profound modeling for the client, assuming they have an awareness of this eros. In our experience, when eros is present, the client knows it, even if it is at a preconscious level. They may lack the words with which to label or describe it, but they often can intuit the presence of this added dynamic.

Therefore, the therapist must monitor, on an on-going basis, his or her ability to allow for the presence of eros while, at the same time, containing it. Receiving supervision can be extremely helpful, as well as being able to share such experiences within the confines of a collegial support group.

One case, in particular, best exemplifies how eros can be a positive therapeutic tool when the therapist learns how to make use of it in a safe and professional manner. Aaron (name changed) came to see one of us, presenting with issues of depression, low self-esteem, career ambivalence and a recently failed relationship. Quite attractive, Aaron responded quickly to the therapy, and reported feeling increased safety within the therapeutic relationship and a higher level of functioning at work and in his personal life. After several months, Aaron began to discuss feeling a growing sense of physical attraction to one of us. Although sharing this attraction, I chose not to disclose my experience to Aaron, believing, from an analytic perspective, that it could interfere with the transference.

In time, I began to feel an increasing sense of ambivalence and confusion over whether to continue working with Aaron. Finally, after much supervision over this case, I recommended to Aaron that we time-limit the work. That is, that we set an actual termination date. I believed, given the situation at the time, that it was the most responsible thing to do, to finish the work, before my judgment became impaired. I justified this recommendation on the basis that Aaron had already made significant changes in his life and was reporting less depression and heightened self-esteem.

For Aaron, this recommendation was devastating. The following week he came to the session despondent and confused. He could not understand why I was assessing the work as nearly finished, when he thought it was just beginning. He talked about feeling hurt and abandoned by yet another man. Clearly, it had triggered in him past, unresolved issues of loss, especially of important male figures in his life. In listening to him, I realized quickly that my recommendation had been unsound and dishonoring of our relationship. It was clearly about my own countertransference, and more precisely, about a belief that I, as

Aaron's therapist, would not be able to continue to provide him with a safe container. I had felt that somehow my personal interests would override my ability to serve him in an effective and fully professional capacity. In short, I was greatly underestimating my ability to stay in a place of professionalism. As well, I was potentially denying Aaron the right to continue his work with me, learning to feel safe and to trust another man who, in this case, would not eventually abandon him.

It took many more sessions to undo the damage and to help Aaron rebuild his trust in me and confidence in my work. First, I had to admit to Aaron that my recommendation had been a poor decision. Second, I needed to reassure him that our work would continue for as long as he needed my assistance. Third, I chose to disclose my attraction to him (giving him enough information to validate his perceptions, but not offering so much that would change the focus of the work). Finally, I needed to explore how such an experience had helped me become a better therapist. I learned from this experience how to contain my attractions to clients so that they would not interfere, overtly or subtly, with my work. In this example, I found that once it was spoken, that is, once the eros was named, it lost some of its charge. Thus, I felt in control of the situation and the therapeutic relationship.

DUAL RELATIONSHIPS

Finally, there is the boundary issue of dual relationships, both during therapy and post-termination. When, if ever, are such relationships acceptable? Akamatsu (1988) identified eight factors therapists should consider before getting involved with clients in a dual capacity: (1) Time since termination, (2) Transference issues, (3) Length of therapy, (4) Nature of the therapy, (5) Nature of termination, (6) Freedom of choice, (7) Whether therapy may be reactivated, and (8) Whether there is harm to the client's welfare. Akamatsu is clearly referring to boundary issues in relationships with former clients, and his recommendations are pertinent for our discussion. First, many therapists engage in post-termination friendships and also believe that under certain circumstances these friendships are acceptable (Salisbury & Kinnier, 1996). As well, another important factor that should be considered in boundary issues is the client diagnosis. The diagnosis should help the therapist assess the ego strength and integrity of the client. Certainly clients with Axis II diagnoses would be poor candidates for the therapist to attempt more fluid boundaries.

There has been much attention paid to the issue of dual relationships between therapist and client in the literature. Thus this chapter will not explore in detail the more extensive issue of client/therapist relationship or post-termination friendships. What we want to focus on, however, are the dual relationships that are unavoidable in a small community.

It has been our experience that the majority of our clients can manage the dual relationship of client and acquaintance. Most of them understand and can maintain the delicate balance required of the more expanded definition of the relationship. Furthermore, our experience has demonstrated that this view of the relationship rarely interferes with the client's willingness and capability to return to the confines of the therapeutic relationship. One of the main determinants of the successful resumption of therapy is the therapist's ability to always maintain the client's confidentiality, not only in regard to issues in therapy, but also to the client's participation in therapy.

Of course, there are those therapists who will argue that a friendship or acquaintance with a client interferes with the transference. In this view, the "container" of the therapeutic relationship is permanently broken. This position, unquestionably, has validity and we do not mean to imply that one can broaden the therapeutic relationship with all clients. There are definitely clients that require the safety and stability of the therapist's office and who cannot handle the disruption of the transference.

In the book *The Road Less Traveled,* (1978) Scott Peck explains that he does not believe in separating his private and professional lives. Although he is speaking of family and friends, thus approaching the issue from another angle, his position indirectly addresses the issues of transference and dual relationships. He believes that he should not withhold his services and wisdom from those close to him, anymore than he would from a paying client. He also admits that this practice is not an easily achieved goal. In spite of that, it is a goal worth striving for, one that requires great effort, intensity, and self-discipline to accomplish. Again, the therapist must use his or her own judgment to determine the appropriateness of the relationship.

CONCLUSION AND RECOMMENDATIONS

The following is a list of practical suggestions gay therapists can use to help navigate through the sometimes uncharted waters of boundary issues.

Diversify one's practice: In working with a variety of populations, rather than just gay men or women, the therapist expands his/her professional field of vision.

Develop a spiritual practice: Recognizing that one's work as a therapist can be a part of one's spiritual path, therapists can stay cognizant of the sacredness of the work that helps therapists to understand their role in creating and maintaining the work. Spiritual practice can involve many different approaches, including meditation.

Break the isolation: By talking to other professionals in the field about boundary issues, therapists can stay aware of the tendency to create dual relationships. One way of doing this is to participate in a support group for gay therapists. For therapists where such support is not so readily available, consider using the Internet to communicate with other therapists about boundary issues.

Get involved in outside activities: An active life helps us keep our priorities clear. Outside activities can include a whole variety of options, including reading, cooking, gardening, running, skiing, etc.

Accept one's humanness: Remember that you're not just a gay therapist. You're also a gay man or lesbian with a full spectrum of human needs.

Rely upon your good judgment: Using one's own intuition to determine the mental health needs of clients when considering redefining boundaries. Trusting in your own ability to set appropriate boundaries when the situation necessitates.

Do your own work: You must be in a therapeutic process yourself to identify and work on your own issues. Therapists must continue to be vigilant in the identification of their countertransference reactions to clients. This can best be accomplished by being or having been in therapy oneself.

Obtain competent supervision: Either with a more experienced therapist, or in a peer supervisory situation, this is one of the most important ways to identify one's own issues relating to the client and to insure responsible behavior.

REFERENCES

Akamatsu, T.J. (1988). Intimate relationships with former clients: National survey of attitudes and behavior among practitioners. *Professional Psychology: Research and Practice*, 19, 454-458.

Allen, M., & Edwards, D. M. (1997). Wilderness treatment: A journey of discovery. *Treatment Today*, 9(1), 14-17.

American Association of Counseling and Development. (1981). Ethical standards. Falls Church, VA, Author.

American Counseling Association (1993, October). ACA proposed standards of practice and ethical standards. *Guidepost*, pp. 15-22.

American Psychological Association (1992). Ethical principles of psychologists and code of conduct. Washington, DC: Author.

Borys, D.S. (1988). Dual relationships between therapist and client: A national survey of clinicians' attitudes and behaviors. Unpublished doctoral dissertation, University of California, Los Angeles.

Borys, D.S., & Pope, K.S. (1989). Dual relationships between therapist and client: A national study of psychologists, psychiatrists and social workers. *Professional Psychology: Research and Practice*, 20.

Cadwell, S. A. (1994). Over-identification with HIV clients. *Journal of Gay & Lesbian Psychotherapy*, 2(2), 77-99.

Corey, C. (1985). Theory and practice of group counseling. California State University, Monterey, CA.

Green, G. D. (1996). When a therapist breaks the rules. *Women & Therapy*, 18, 1-10.

Heyward, C. (1994). When boundaries betray us. San Francisco, Harper.

Kitchener, K. S. (1988). Dual role relationships: What makes them so problematic? *Journal of Counseling and Development*, 67, 217-221.

Kooden, H. (1994). The gay male therapist as an agent of socialization. *Journal of Gay & Lesbian Psychotherapy*, 2, 39-64.

Lease, S. H., Cogdal, P. A., & Smith, D. (1995). Counseling expectancies related to counselors' sexual orientation and clients' internalized homophobia. *Journal of Gay & Lesbian Psychotherapy*, 2(3), 51-65.

Lima, G., Lo Presto, C. T., Sherman, M. F., & Sobelman, S. A. (1993). The relationship between homophobia and self-esteem in gay males with AIDS. *Journal of Homosexuality*, 25(4), 69-76.

Meyers, D. (1997). Outward bound to wilderness treatment. *Treatment Today*, 9(1), 17.

Peck, M. S. (1978). The road less traveled. New York: Simon and Schuster.

Pope, K. S., Tabachnick, B. G., & Keith-Spiegel, P. (1987). Ethics of practice: The beliefs and behaviors of psychologists and therapists. *American Psychologist*, 42, 993-1006.

Purtilo, R., & Sorrell, J. (1986). The ethical dilemmas of a rural physician. *Hastings Center Report, 16*(4), 24-28.

Regehr, C., & Glancy, G. (1995). Sexual exploitation of patients: Issues for colleagues. *American Journal of Orthopsychiatry,* 65(2), 194-202.

Salisbury, W. A., & Kinnier, R. T. (1996). Posttermination friendship between counselors and clients. *Journal of Counseling and Development,* 74, 495-500.

Schoel, J., Pruty, D., & Radcliffe, P. (1996). Experiential therapy: Adventure-based counseling. *Islands of Healing,* 185.

Schwartz, R. D. (1989). When the therapist is gay: Personal and clinical reflections. *Journal of Gay & Lesbian Psychotherapy,* 1, 41-51.

Treatment Planning
for Gay and Lesbian Clients

Christopher J. Alexander

SUMMARY. Oftentimes gays and lesbians enter psychotherapy unclear about the eventual goals they want to attain. Without a clear understanding of what gays and lesbians want out of therapy, both therapist and client can feel at times that the treatment is unfocused and haphazard. The development of realistic treatment plans by private practitioners is also taking on more importance in this era of managed care. When therapists take the time to help clients define the goals they want to achieve by coming to therapy, the treatment feels more focused and effective to all parties. Guidelines for developing treatment plans for gay and lesbian clients are offered. *[Article copies available for a fee from The Haworth Document Delivery Service: 1-800-342-9678. E-mail address: getinfo@haworthpressinc.com]*

INTRODUCTION

It has been estimated that between 25 and 75% of gay men and lesbians receive counseling at some point in their adult lives (Bradford, Ryan, & Rothblum, 1994; Morgan, 1992; Rudolph, 1988). Most studies indicate that lesbians are more likely to seek counseling than are gay men, with 63% receiving this support from a private counselor.

Whereas many people seek psychotherapy for specific issues or life

Christopher J. Alexander, PhD, is a licensed clinical psychologist in Santa Fe, NM. He can be reached at 620-B W. San Francisco Street, Santa Fe, NM 87501.

[Haworth co-indexing entry note]: "Treatment Planning for Gay and Lesbian Clients." Alexander, Christopher J. Co-published simultaneously in *Journal of Gay & Lesbian Social Services* (The Haworth Press, Inc.) Vol. 8, No. 4, 1998, pp. 95-106; and: *Working with Gay Men and Lesbians in Private Psychotherapy Practice* (ed: Christopher J. Alexander) The Haworth Press, Inc., 1998, pp. 95-106. Single or multiple copies of this article are available for a fee from The Haworth Document Delivery Service [1-800-342-9678, 9:00 a.m. - 5:00 p.m. (EST). E-mail address: getinfo@haworthpressinc.com].

events–relationship problems, coping with loss, substance abuse–there are others who come to therapy mainly to address matters related to personal growth. Gay men and lesbians may fit this latter category more so than others since gay men and lesbians typically have unique feelings and life circumstances, mainly related to personal identity and adjustment to being a sexual minority. Therefore, when many gay men and women come to therapy, rather than stating clear reasons or objectives for seeking treatment, they will report simply that they desire to find out who they are.

In many respects, it can be easier working with the client who wants to focus on specific areas of their life. If someone indicates, for example, they are depressed or are trying to find ways of coping with past trauma or abuse, there are a variety of widely-known and accepted interventions and techniques. Even in those cases where a client presents with a concern that is unfamiliar to a particular psychotherapist–coping with employment discrimination, for example–most clinicians can turn to the literature or to a colleague for guidance and advice.

On the other hand, when gay or lesbian clients come to therapy for the first time, and are expressing their needs in vague, non-specific ways, it can be confusing for some therapists knowing where to focus the treatment. As psychotherapists in these situations, we may wonder if we should take the initiative and encourage disclosure about family of origin, coming out, homophobia, sexuality, or the myriad of other topics that gay and lesbian clients often address.

Regardless of whether clients come to therapy with specified goals in mind, it is helpful for therapists to think in terms of treatment planning. Treatment planning includes taking into account the therapist's clinical theory and style, the immediate needs of the client, and the short and long-term goals of the client. The care therapists put into this process can prevent problems and misunderstandings in the future, and increase the likelihood of a successful outcome for the client.

Treatment planning, as conceptualized in this article, is a collaborative process between therapist and client. It is a useful technique for most therapists, independent of theoretical approach or treatment style. The goal of treatment planning is to help the therapist stay mindful of what it is the client wants out of psychotherapy, regardless of what issues or themes are being addressed on a session by session basis.

BASIC CONSIDERATIONS IN TREATMENT PLANNING

Initial Contact

Since initial contact between therapist and client typically occurs over the phone, each brings impressions about the other to the first session. Therefore, how therapists present themselves over the phone with prospective clients is an important factor. As Karpel (1994) points out, treatment begins before the first session, before actually meeting the client.

Most therapists do a mini-evaluation over the telephone, thus giving them some idea as to whether they are the one best suited to address the caller's issues and concerns. For their part, potential clients present their first test of the therapist over the phone, gauging whether they like the therapist, can feel safe with him or her, whether they trust the person, and if they feel the therapist can help them. Therefore, if the client shows to his or her appointment, it is probable that the therapist passed this first test.

How therapists present themselves during the initial phone call will affect any and all subsequent treatment. Because of this, it is important for therapists to know their style and preferences of relating to potential clients over the phone. For example, therapists can ask themselves the following:

- How do you feel about self-disclosure during the first phone call? What are your range of responses when callers ask if you are gay or lesbian?
- How do you explain what therapy is–and how you work–for those callers who are unfamiliar with psychotherapy?
- What information do you feel you need to have before scheduling an appointment with a caller? In what ways do you obtain this information?
- What information do you feel the caller must have about you and your practice of psychotherapy before scheduling an initial appointment?

Clients inevitably remember their impressions of initial phone contact with therapists. Because of this, it is important to handle intake phone calls with courtesy and respect, and to communicate genuine interest in the caller. It is a mistake to think that initial phone contact with prospective clients is solely a time for scheduling an appointment. Both client and therapist need to have ample time for addressing key topics before setting up a face-to-face meeting.

Therapists differ with regard to how much information to obtain from prospective clients over the phone. Though there are no firm guidelines on this, the minimal requirement should be that both the therapist and the caller feel that an initial appointment is worth the caller's time and money. As trained professionals, most experienced therapists should be able to determine in the course of a phone call whether scheduling an appointment or referring the caller to another practitioner is warranted after listening to the caller's questions and concerns.

The First Session

A collaborative relationship between the therapist and the client is a vital component of any successful therapy. If the client is not engaged in the process of treatment, all interventions on the part of the therapist will be reduced in effectiveness.

While this seems to be relevant to almost every type of therapy client, it is especially true with gay and lesbian clients. Many, if not most, sexual minority clients bring common fears or concerns to therapy. Therefore, gays and lesbians entering psychotherapy will typically ask themselves the following questions:

- Will this therapist see me as abnormal because of my sexual preference?
- Will this therapist try to change my sexual orientation?
- Can this therapist understand what it is like being a sexual minority?
- Has this therapist had experience working with other gay and lesbian clients?
- What are this therapist's views on the origins and treatment of homosexuality?
- Can I trust this therapist?

In light of this, many gay and lesbian clients approach new therapists with great caution. It is not uncommon, for example, for gay and lesbian clients to pose a series of conscious and unconscious tests (Engel & Ferguson, 1990) that therapists must pass before they start to trust and disclose to this person. Because many sexual minorities have been treated poorly by family, friends and society, they expect that therapists will hold negative opinions about them. Conversely, many expect out-right rejection from the therapist. Some clients will therefore prematurely terminate psychotherapy, fearing that if they don't, the therapist will.

This is why it is important to establish rapport with gay and lesbian clients early on in the psychotherapy process. Regardless of one's theoretical orientation or approach to doing psychotherapy, failure to address clients' ambivalence, fears and questions early on in therapy will often result in a negative experience for the client.

The initial session with new clients is a process of socialization. In essence, we are teaching clients how we work, what we expect from them, and what we have to offer. Though unconditional positive regard, empathic listening, and reflective statements are part of our initial work with new clients, it is also important that we attempt to address the fears and questions they have. Sometimes it can be helpful to ask, "What fears or concerns do you have about being in psychotherapy?"

Part of the responsibility psychotherapists carry is to assess whether a particular client is suited for psychotherapy, and if so, which approach will best serve this individual. This is where therapists use the most complex of all therapeutic skills. As Malan (1990) points out, interviewing therapists must simultaneously "think psychiatrically, psychodynamically, psychotherapeutically, and practically" (p. 210).

In order to achieve this, therapists must be very open and honest with clients about a variety of topic areas:

- *Basic Rules.* Therapists differ with regard to how long therapy appointments last, how fees should be handled, cancellation policies, etc. Each of these points should be addressed with new clients before the conclusion of the first session. If therapists do time-limited therapy, this should also be clarified with clients early on.

- *Nature of the Treatment.* Clients need to be told whether a therapist's style of doing therapy is interactive, analytical, will involve role-play or homework, whether significant others in the client's life must attend, etc. When clients know this information in advance, they are less likely to misinterpret the manner and therapeutic style of the therapist.

- *Acknowledge Experience.* Whether therapists should inform gay and lesbian clients of their own sexual orientation is a controversial issue. Depending upon a therapist's theoretical orientation and own privacy needs, some opt to disclose their sexuality while others choose not to. Regardless of how one handles this topic with new clients, it is still necessary to communicate one's experience of working with gay and lesbian clients. Even if they do not ask, most gay and lesbian clients will wonder about the therapist's professional experience with other sexual minority clients. By acknowledging one's familiarity and experience in working with gay and lesbian clients, therapists help to alleviate much of the client's concerns.

- *Assurances of Safety.* Gays and lesbians have experienced victimization most of their lives. For some this has been from outright violence and abuse. For others it has taken the form of teasing, name-calling and self-doubt. Because of this, gay and lesbian clients require assurance from the therapist that he or she will not harm them, ridicule them, violate their personal boundaries, or subject them to harm.

After the initial session, it is necessary for the therapist to evaluate the quality of relationship he or she feels it is possible to have with the client. Ultimately, the first consideration in deciding upon any course of treatment involves the quality of alliance the therapist feels with the client. This includes how the therapist feels about the client, as well as how the client feels about the therapist. In order for there to be the possibility of a strong working alliance, both therapist and client must feel they are able to work together. As therapists, this is where we need to pay particular attention to our countertransference issues during the initial session with clients.

Defining Goals

At some point during, or shortly after, the initial session with a client, therapists should be thinking about what treatment goals are important for a particular client. Some clients are able to be very clear about what their goals are. For example, they might tell the therapist they need support around coming out to a particular person. As mentioned earlier, however, many gay and lesbian clients come to therapy unable to express what it is they want to achieve other than with general terms such as better self-esteem, higher self-confidence, or dating skills.

Goals provide both therapist and client with a sense of direction. Without a mutual idea of what goals the client has for him or herself, therapy can feel fragmented and disjointed. This can be particularly true with those clients who come to therapy and consistently report on their lives. Though it can be argued that some clients may require the opportunity to vent about their daily lives, for many others this is resistance aimed at deterring more focused, in-depth, and goal-directed work.

Discussing goals with clients allows the therapist to clarify any misunderstanding the client has about mental health treatment. Further, both therapist and client learn one another's expectations about the treatment. An example is where the therapist expects clients to do journaling, homework, or other kinds of out-of-session exercises. When clients understand that this is one way the therapist helps his or her clients achieve their goals, they are less resistant to the suggestion of these techniques when they arise.

Focusing on goals also helps to make psychotherapy clients feel more hopeful about what therapy can do for them. Many clients mistakenly believe that change and growth is simply a matter of therapists asking questions for the client to respond to. Though this may be the preferred technique of some therapists, without an understanding of where this type of interaction is heading, little progress in the client's life can be expected.

Goals are best viewed as the foundation of psychotherapy. Ultimately, clients need to be able to discuss whatever is important to them, and therapists should feel at liberty to use whatever modality they are trained in and therefore comfortable with. But with a mutual understanding of why the client is in treatment, what he or she expects from therapy, and how the therapist intends on helping the client in this direction, therapy feels less haphazard.

One additional benefit of discussing goals with clients is that it reinforces the therapeutic alliance and gives clients a sense of participation in their treatment. When clients are able to articulate their goals, they realize that the therapist can guide them toward change in their lives, but that ultimately, the achievement of these goals rests with them. In turn, they learn that they have control of their own lives.

Finally, defining goals early in psychotherapy makes it easier for both client and therapist when issues of termination arise. Instead of the therapist having to ask general questions such as, "How do you feel therapy went for you?," the therapist and client can assess in greater depth to what extent the client was able to achieve his or her goals through the process of psychotherapy. This is particularly noteworthy when clients indicate to the therapist their feeling that the treatment simply isn't working.

Assisting Clients with Defining Goals

As mentioned, many gay and lesbian clients may not be able to articulate their motives or goals for entering psychotherapy. For some, all they know is they need help, a reality check, or some guidance on how to feel good about being a sexual minority.

With these kinds of clients, the idea of setting goals can feel to some therapists like they are imposing an agenda on the client. An alternate way of looking at this, however, is to view the defining of treatment goals as a mutual effort at taking control of the direction of the therapy. Also, treatment goals don't always have to be seen in behavioral terms, such as is common with habits such as smoking. Rather, goals can also be set for more broad or existential issues and questions which clients often present.

Sometime during the initial session, it can be helpful to ask clients, "What do you want your life to look like when you and I have finished working together?" Alternately, clients can be asked, "What clues will you look for to know that you're getting what you want from coming to see me?" This challenges clients to think in terms of both process and outcome. Certainly, these questions don't have to be fully answered during the first session, and in some cases, may even turn into content for discussion in following sessions. One client and I spent several sessions addressing his responses to these questions, as they brought up for him issues of dependency, taking control, autonomy, and initiative. This then became the initial focus of our work together. One result of this was that instead of him expecting me to tell him when to come out to his parents, he defined one of his initial goals that he would make this decision.

In light of this, it is important that clients take an active role in defining their goals for therapy. This doesn't mean that therapists don't offer alternative suggestions, or encourage more realistic expectations. Rather, when goals are defined in the client's own words and vocabulary, the client is more invested in the attainment of these goals, and often feels better able to achieve them.

Integrating Goals into a Treatment Plan

Once the client and therapist have a mutual understanding of what it is the client wants out of coming to psychotherapy, the therapist must then think in terms of how these goals can be achieved. Behavioral therapists typically break goals into small, manageable steps clients can take to meet them. Other therapists will need to think in terms of their own modality, and how their theory and technique looks at specific outcomes in psychotherapy. Again, identifying and working toward goals in psychotherapy does not have to conflict with most theoretical orientations and approaches.

Just because a client has established a particular goal–learning how to date, for example–doesn't mean that therapists focus all their initial efforts toward helping the client achieve this particular goal. Rather, some gay and lesbian clients will lack fundamental skill, experience, or understanding about many areas of gay life, and therapists must factor this in to the treatment. Otherwise, the client may fail at attaining their goals, and the therapist will have failed at anticipating this fact.

This is where clinicians are challenged to use their professional experience and insight in order to foresee which other issues clients may first need to address. By having a broader perspective than the clients on how sexual identity affects the goals clients set for themselves, the therapist can bring this into the treatment.

For example, let's presume that a client has stated that he or she wants to make it a treatment goal to learn how to date others, with the idea that hopefully he or she can find a permanent partner. If the therapist simply educates the client about ways to meet other gay men or lesbians–while suggesting some do's and don'ts about dating–he or she may be doing the client a disservice. This is based on the perspective that therapists need to acquaint themselves with the client's history, experience and belief system as it pertains to being gay or lesbian before pursuing the treatment goal in its entirety.

The therapist in the above example will first want to find out the client's prior experience with dating and relationships, in order to ascertain the client's readiness for and familiarity with gay dating patterns. It might also be helpful to know what beliefs the client has about gay relationships. Many gay men and lesbians believe that long-term relationships with other gay men or women simply are not possible. This will certainly color the clients' perceptions as they date. Finally, some therapists will want to find out about the client's family of origin, to determine how relationships were modeled for the individual as he or she was growing up.

With this in mind, the therapist can tell the client that he or she is willing to work with them on achieving their goals, but that they would first like to spend some time exploring the client's sexual and relationship history, as well as their overall feelings and beliefs about homosexuality.

Therapists have a responsibility for assessing how clients feel about the fact that they are gay or lesbian, as well as testing the perceptions sexual minorities have about homosexuality. This is especially noteworthy with regard to internalized homophobia, the adoption of negative societal attitudes about homosexuality by the homosexual person. McDermott et al. (1989), for example, reported that gay men and lesbians' internalized homophobia was the best predictor of their overall comfort in discussing certain topics when they did not know their counselor's sexual orientation. Conversely, Lease et al. (1995) found that individuals who had internalized fewer of society's negative messages about homosexuality had more positive expectations about their own role (i.e., motivation, openness, responsibility) in therapy.

Managed Care

Increasingly, the public is being offered employer-based insurance coverage through managed care companies. In this model, health care professionals must typically get prior approval for offering treatment to a patient. In the area of mental health, for example, a care manager designated by the managed care company will authorize a certain number of psychotherapy sessions. The psychotherapist can request that additional sessions be covered, though the approval of this is at the discretion of the care manager.

Fortunately, a substantial number of managed care firms ask their providers (1) if they specialize in working with sexual minorities, and (2) if they wish to be identified as gay or lesbian. This allows for the potential of a better "fit" between client and therapist. As can be surmised, however, many potential clients are reluctant to tell their insurance company that they seek psychological treatment for issues related to their sexual identity. Thus, they may or may not get a therapist who is sensitive to gay and lesbian mental health issues.

A particularly challenging circumstance for both client and therapist is when the managed care company requires information about why the client is seeking treatment. Most managed care firms work under the philosophy that psychotherapy should be focused on specific concerns, not the more general category of personal growth. This requires that therapists communicate some details about why the client is coming to therapy, and what mode of intervention is being utilized.

Whether or not to disclose to a managed care company that a client is dealing with issues related to sexual orientation is a clinical issue that should be discussed between the client and the mental health professional. Ultimately, the client's wishes should dictate how this disclosure is handled. In general, without adequate substantiation on the therapist's part as to why continued psychotherapy is warranted, the care manager will likely restrict the total number of therapy sessions available to the client.

If both the therapist and the client agree that psychotherapy is indicated, and that disclosure of the client's mental health concerns are necessary, there may be limits to the amount of confidentiality the client can be guaranteed.

CONCLUSION

Gay men and lesbians will continue to be consumers of mental health services, even as societal acceptance of homosexuality increases. The issues confronting sexual minorities are reflective of the cultural changes our community is experiencing, from gay and lesbian parents to "out" adolescents. Whether it be in the form of individual, group, or couples treatment, many gay men and lesbians will find they can achieve fuller acceptance of their sexuality through the professional services of a psychotherapist.

By keeping treatment goals in mind, therapists can find that their work with sexual minorities is more fulfilling, focused, and effective. Introducing goals to psychotherapy clients also communicates our genuine interest in wanting to help them have the lives and happiness they desire.

REFERENCES

Bradford, J., Ryan, C., & Rothblum, E.D. (1994). National lesbian health care survey: Implications for mental health care. *Journal of Consulting and Clinical Psychology*, 62 (2), 228-242.

Engel, L., & Ferguson, T. (1990). *Imaginary crimes: Why we punish ourselves and how to stop*. Boston: Houghton Mifflin Company.

Karpel, M.A. (1994). *Evaluating couples: A handbook for practitioners*. New York: W.W. Norton and Company.

Lease, S., Cogdal, P.A., & Smith, D. (1995). Counseling expectancies related to counselors' sexual orientation and clients' internalized homophobia. *Journal of Gay & Lesbian Psychotherapy*, 2 (3), 51-65.

Malan, D. H. (1990). *Individual psychotherapy and the science of psychodynamics*. London: Butterworths.

McDermott, D., Tyndall, L., & Lichtenberg, J.W. (1989). Factors related to counselor preference among gays and lesbians. *Journal of Counseling and Development*, 68, 31-35.

Morgan, K.S. (1992). Caucasian lesbians' use of psychotherapy: A matter of attitude? *Psychology of Women Quarterly*, 16, 127-130.

Rudolph, J. (1988). Counselors' attitude toward homosexuality: A selective review of the literature. *Journal of Counseling and Development*, 67, 165-168.

Index

Acquired Immune Deficiency
     Syndrome (AIDS) 16-17,61, 83-84
Aging, gays, lesbians and 17-18

Bisexuality 7, 64
Boundaries, professional 45-46,50-51,
     72-73,77-78,79,89

Coming out 11,48,55,64-65,67,78-81
Continuing education, for therapists
     15-16
Countertransference, in therapy 52,70,
     83-85
Couples, lesbian and gay 17

Freud, S. 9

Gender role 63-64
Goal setting, in therapy 100-104

Homophobia 12,18,52-53,64,65,71

Identity development, gay and lesbian
     61-62,66-68

Managed care 30-31,104-105
Market, private practice 30,32-41

Religion 65-66

Shame 12,18
Small towns, psychotherapy in 44-45,
     81-82
Substance abuse 9,48

Termination, from therapy 51
Transference, in therapy 51-52,71
Treatment planning 96-106

Haworth
DOCUMENT DELIVERY
SERVICE

This valuable service provides a single-article order form for any article from a Haworth journal.

- *Time Saving:* No running around from library to library to find a specific article.
- *Cost Effective:* All costs are kept down to a minimum.
- *Fast Delivery:* Choose from several options, including same-day FAX.
- *No Copyright Hassles:* You will be supplied by the original publisher.
- *Easy Payment:* Choose from several easy payment methods.

Open Accounts Welcome for ...
- Library Interlibrary Loan Departments
- Library Network/Consortia Wishing to Provide Single-Article Services
- Indexing/Abstracting Services with Single Article Provision Services
- Document Provision Brokers and Freelance Information Service Providers

---

MAIL or *FAX* THIS ENTIRE ORDER FORM TO:

Haworth Document Delivery Service
The Haworth Press, Inc.
10 Alice Street
Binghamton, NY 13904-1580

or FAX: 1-800-895-0582
or CALL: 1-800-429-6784
9am-5pm EST

PLEASE SEND ME PHOTOCOPIES OF THE FOLLOWING SINGLE ARTICLES:
1) Journal Title: _____

    Vol/Issue/Year:_____Starting & Ending Pages:_____

Article Title:_____

_____

2) Journal Title: _____

    Vol/Issue/Year:_____Starting & Ending Pages:_____

Article Title:_____

_____

3) Journal Title: _____

    Vol/Issue/Year:_____Starting & Ending Pages:_____

Article Title:_____

_____

4) Journal Title: _____

    Vol/Issue/Year:_____Starting & Ending Pages:_____

Article Title:_____

_____

(See other side for Costs and Payment Information)

COSTS: Please figure your cost to order quality copies of an article.

1. Set-up charge per article: $8.00
   ($8.00 × number of separate articles) _____

2. Photocopying charge for each article:

   1-10 pages: $1.00 _____

   11-19 pages: $3.00 _____

   20-29 pages: $5.00 _____

   30+ pages: $2.00/10 pages _____

3. Flexicover (optional): $2.00/article _____

4. Postage & Handling: US: $1.00 for the first article/
   $.50 each additional article _____

   Federal Express: $25.00 _____

   Outside US: $2.00 for first article/
   $.50 each additional article _____

5. Same-day FAX service: $.50 per page _____

   GRAND TOTAL: _____

METHOD OF PAYMENT: (please check one)

❏ Check enclosed ❏ Please ship and bill. PO # _____
(sorry we can ship and bill to bookstores only! All others must pre-pay)

❏ Charge to my credit card: ❏ Visa; ❏ MasterCard; ❏ Discover;
❏ American Express;

Account Number: _____ Expiration date: _____

Signature: *X* _____

Name: _____ Institution: _____

Address: _____

_____

City: _____ State: _____ Zip: _____

Phone Number: _____ FAX Number: _____

MAIL or *FAX* THIS ENTIRE ORDER FORM TO:

Haworth Document Delivery Service	**or FAX:** 1-800-895-0582
The Haworth Press, Inc.	**or CALL:** 1-800-429-6784
10 Alice Street	(9am-5pm EST)
Binghamton, NY 13904-1580	

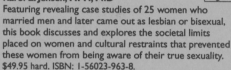

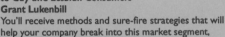